Freight Dog

The Dark Side of Aviation

by

Kimber C. Turner

Table of Contents

Foreword

Foreword

It was the best of jobs, it was the worst of jobs. At least that is how Charles Dickens would have described his career as an airline pilot.

It's like that old joke we have all heard about the poor sap working for the airlines tossing baggage outside in the winter, slipping on the snow and ice, complaining about the difficult conditions when a coworker asks him why he doesn't just quit. He responds, "What, and get out of aviation?"

Aviation does that. It gets in your blood. It's addictive. Once you have been bitten by it, you don't want to give it up or do anything else. At the same time it can be a cruel task master. It makes demands on your time and energy promising travel and excitement but doesn't always deliver on its promises or even pay a livable wage in some cases. Of course, there are those few flying jobs with travel to exotic locations and really (and I mean really) good pay. I know because I had one once until my gravy train pulled into the station and I had to get off.

The term freight dog used in the title has been a part of aviation terminology almost from the beginning of the airline industry. It was originally a derogatory term for a pilot who flew freight, typically in older aircraft no longer used by the passenger carriers. If you were a freight dog, you were at the bottom of the pilot food chain. As a freight dog, your airplanes were old and greasy. You didn't get to walk through the passenger terminal in your uniform and enjoy the celebrity status that was afforded the typical airline pilot and you probably flew at night and didn't make as much money.

That was then. Today's freight dog does OK if he's flying for one of the larger overnight package companies. Of course, he still flies at night for the most part, hence the reference to the dark side of aviation in the title but apart from just the nighttime aspect, aviation does have a dark side and depending on the airline, it could be a very dark side. It has to do with the unpleasant, frustrating and sometimes disastrous situations and conditions brought about by the decisions and policies of the inept or misguided executives and managers who somehow find their way into positions beyond the scope of their ability and intelligence. While that part of my aviation experience may have been very uncomfortable, it does make for a good story.

Other than when discussing a public figure, the names have been altered to protect the innocent, which is me. After all, even though the courts have consistently held that truth is the ultimate defense, why run the risk of having to spend money defending yourself from frivolous law suits filed by thin skinned tyrants who for their entire careers have mistreated the truth as badly as they have the underlings they abused.

Chapter One

You Gotta Start Somewhere

The second grader looked at the paste sticks and construction paper that his art class had been working with. He realized that the model airplane he had seen just a few days earlier had been constructed from similar materials and it gave him an idea.

That evening sitting at the kitchen table without benefit of blueprints or plans of any kind, he set about constructing a model airplane of his own with the generous supply of paste sticks and construction paper he had secured from his art class. He looked at his finished product and was pleased. His second grade teacher, Mrs. Spaulding, wouldn't have been as pleased as he, had she known of his acquisition.

His interest in aviation had been sparked just a couple of weeks earlier when his father had taken him to the local airport for a ride in a single engine airplane to do some sight seeing and view their house from the air. During the course of the flight, the pilot had allowed the second grader to take the controls and make a turn thus beginning a love affair with airplanes that would last the rest of his life.

I didn't realize until years later that what I had done is technically considered theft. A twinge of guilt still rears its ugly head when I think of it. Mrs. Spaulding, if you are reading this I apologize and if memory serves, I may have borrowed a jar of paste as well.

It was about fifty years from that first flight to my last and I got the same thrill each time the tower cleared me for takeoff and I pushed the throttles forward in the Airbus A-300 that I flew for the last few years of my career.

Of course you don't start out flying a heavy, wide body, transport category aircraft but the goal of tens of thousands of pilots is to ultimately fly for an airline. There are many paths that lead to that airline job. In the past the airlines had an ample supply of military aviators to choose from but these days it is more common for a prospective airline pilot to have come up through the general aviation ranks. A pilot will typically get their instructor rating and teach flying to build up hours and eventually find a job flying corporate aircraft until their experience will meet the requirements of the airlines.

My path was a little different. I had acquired my licenses and ratings including my instructor rating and was fully expecting to start giving flight instruction to build time when I got a call from the gentleman who owned the flight school I had attended. He told me that a local commuter airline was looking for a copilot and that he had recommended me. I went to the interview the day I turned 27 and received the best birthday present ever in the form of a job offer. The excitement of having become a professional pilot would have to serve me well because the pay was nothing to get excited about. My starting salary was a whopping one hundred fifty dollars a week before taxes.

Almost immediately I started writing to the major carriers. As a prospective airline pilot I understood that you didn't really get to pick the airline you wanted to fly for. You applied to all of them and took every interview you could get and if an offer came along you accepted it and were thankful. The first couple of interviews were generally expected to be for practice since the national average was about three and a half interviews before getting hired.

What my youthful enthusiasm didn't allow me to realize at the time was that my resume, with its pitifully small amount of flight time, was probably the cause of several stomach cramps resulting from the laughter it must have generated in the various human resources departments that received it.

Ignorance is bliss of course so I wasn't deterred by my lack of any real experience. I just continued sending out resumes and filling out applications. In my mind, it was a fitting tribute to my perseverance when some nine months later I received a letter from Delta Airlines offering an interview. Those around me with more flight time and still no offers from the airlines were somewhat less enthusiastic.

I arrived in Atlanta at the appointed time for the interview carrying my log book in which I had dutifully logged every one of my measly little nine hundred and some odd hours of flight time. The interview process at Delta consisted of a records check, a battery of psychological tests and a visit with the psychologist before actually interviewing with someone from the flight department. Those lucky enough to make it through all of that would be called back for a physical.

Rumor had it that the psychologist had a rocking chair you would sit in during his portion of the interview. To rock or not to rock; that was the question. The applicants in the waiting room excitedly debated the rocking question and shared stories of their flying experiences. As I listened to the conversations around me I began to realize that someone somewhere had made a terrible mistake.

I was surrounded by former military pilots loaded with experience in sophisticated jet aircraft. With no jet time, I could only assume that my application had been mishandled and accidentally placed in the pile of those to be called for an interview. It was going to be difficult to shine in a crowd of such stellar applicants but I was there so I decided to make the best of it and at least gain some interviewing experience.

After answering hundreds of psychological questions with my number two pencil I reasoned that since I didn't secretly hate my parents, that part of the interview probably went OK. The only question that I can remember the psychologist asking me as I rocked in his chair was how to say "mother" in Hungarian. He had noted that I had been a Hungarian linguist in the Air Force. It was probably the mention of my time in the Air Force listed in my resume that had caused the fortunate fumbling of my application resulting in the interview. Well, that and the fact that I was married with 1.2 children which fit Delta's profile for a suitable applicant.

The representative from the flight department opened my log book and looked at me with an expression that said, "Why are you even here?" That portion of the interview was understandably truncated as the interviewer assured me they would be in touch. I don't really think he said it out loud but what I heard was, "Don't call us, we'll call you."

Two weeks later I received a letter thanking me for my time and regretting that I could not be considered any further. While that was to be expected, the unfortunate problem is that with Delta, once you have been interviewed, that's the end of it. Even with more experience at a later date they will not reconsider you.

It was back to square one for me. I would just keep flying and building time and of course, continue filling out applications. My flight time would eventually reach the level that most of the airlines required but I felt that it would be a benefit for me to have some experience in something a little more sophisticated than what I was currently flying.

The little town I lived in didn't have much to offer in corporate aviation but I had recently stumbled upon a magazine article about Houston's booming general aviation community. With a year of flying under my belt I had earned a week of vacation and decided the best way to use it would be to travel to Houston and pound the pavement in search of a position offering better pay and hopefully in something with jet engines.

Armed with little more than a stack of resumes and a road atlas, I took a flight to Houston and rented a car. My first stop was Atlantic Aviation, a fixed base operator at Hobby Airport. Fixed base operators or FBOs as they are called, are a base of operations for general aviation usually including a terminal, ramp and hangar space for the corporate or charter operators based there, and for transient aircraft as well.

After parking the rental car I walked into the main building at Atlantic Aviation and asked the receptionist where I might find the offices of any corporate flight departments that were based there. She directed me to the second floor where I found six or seven offices with signs on the doors indicating who occupied each office. I started knocking on doors, introducing myself and explaining that I was looking for a pilot position.

The first office I happened upon was Thunderbird Airways which I learned was a Lear Jet charter operator. The secretary graciously accepted my resume but told me she didn't know if they had any openings at that time. I repeated the process visiting several offices and leaving a trail of resumes that could have led Hansel and Gretel home.

A couple of hours into the process I figured I had done all that I could at Atlantic Aviation and decided to go to the next FBO and start all over again. Half way down the hall to the stairs I heard foot steps rapidly approaching from behind me. A female voice asked, "Excuse me sir. Are you Kimber Turner?"

Somewhat surprised I turned and said, "Well, yes, am I famous already?" I only hoped I hadn't offended someone during the course of my canvassing.

"I don't know about that," she said, "but you dropped off your resume and our chief pilot would like to interview you. He's in the office now if you have a few minutes."

With excited relief I thought, "I've got all day if you need" but simply said, "I'd be happy to." As fate would have it, the Lear Jet charter operator in the first office I had visited did indeed have a couple of openings. They offered me a position as a Lear Jet First Officer (copilot) which I accepted. My trip to Houston had paid off big time. I had doubled my salary and would now be flying jet equipment.

I have always said that being at the right place at the right time was the best way to land a job in aviation. Of course it helps if you are willing to traipse half way across the country to be at that right place.

Being half way across the country was going to be my next hurdle. My new employer had scheduled me for a Lear Jet ground school that I would attend in Dallas on my way to Houston. I left Ohio in the dead of winter wearing four layers of clothing and armed with an ice scraper for the inside of my windshield to combat the lack of a heater in my beat up old VW Beetle. Nearing the Texas border, the warming trend allowed me to peel off a couple layers of clothing and abandon my window scraping duties. I was warming to the idea of living in Houston and avoiding the harsh winter weather.

After completing my training and finding an apartment, I had my wife and young daughter come join me in Houston. It didn't take long to settle into my new job.

Flying the Lear Jet was fun and exciting. My schedule consisted of five days of "on call" then a couple of days off. The beepers that we carried in the late seventies seem crude and bulky compared to today's cell phones. When the beeper would buzz we would have to find a pay phone to return the call to the company and receive our assignment. It could be any time, day or night, and you might be anywhere like at the Astrodome in the middle of watching a baseball game when you would be paged and told, "Pack for three days. You're going to New York."

Some of what I found myself doing in the jet charter business was very satisfying, like the trips when we would pick up a heart to be transplanted or an ambulance flight. During one such trip we had transported a young burn victim from a small town in Texas to Houston for special treatment. I later received a letter of appreciation from his thankful mother.

Those types of trips were very rewarding but most of what we did consisted of business and pleasure trips for a clientele that ranged from high level executives to the occasional celebrity. As you may well guess, that type of clientele tended to spend time at some very desirable destinations.

I might find myself flying an important Houston real estate developer to Palm Springs to play golf with Ken Venturi and I would need to lay over in a nice hotel for the week waiting to bring him back. There were trips to the Bahamas and Grand Cayman with vacationing oil company executives.

Oil fueled the booming economy in Houston and played a big part in our charter business. One memorable assignment had me flying Red Adair to Mexico to battle an oil well fire that was out of control. This was a particularly exciting trip for me having seen the movie "Hellfighters" in which John Wayne played the part of Red Adair.

I met Mr. Adair in the lobby of Atlantic Aviation during preparations for the trip. His diminutive physical stature was not what the movie had led me to expect but his personality certainly was. As we made small talk I allowed that I had seen and enjoyed the American Express commercials that he had recently done. He laughed, held out his arm pointing to his watch and said, "They gave me this."

It was a beautiful gold Rolex with an oil derrick made out of diamonds on the face. Not knowing what would be an appropriate comment I simply said, "Wow, that's nice."

He sprinkled his reply with a few expletives saying, "Yeah, well if they ever get around to paying me what they owe me for those commercials I could buy three of these."

It was an honor meeting such a legend and I still have the baseball cap with the Red Adair Company logo that one of his men gave me.

Houston was a boom town with the money flowing about as fast as the oil that supplied it. Everybody that was making money in the oil patch seemed to be spending it on jet charters and we were expected to take exceptional care of our clients. We customized the contents of the bar in the aircraft to meet the personal taste of our passengers and paid attention to every detail of any special catering or other requirements they may have had. In turn, we were treated well, put up in the finest hotels and were afforded an unlimited expense account. It was like a perpetual paid vacation.

My enthusiasm for the airline position that I previously coveted began to diminish as I grew accustomed to luxury hotels and thick juicy steaks. The flow of applications I had been sending to the airlines slowed down to a virtual dribble as I thought to myself, "Other than the pay, why would anyone want to fly for an airline and actually have to work when you could do this for a living?"

Then the oil bubble burst. My permanent paid vacation was about to end. Several of us were called to a meeting at the company headquarters. One by one we were ushered into the chief pilot's office. John, a fellow copilot, returned to the waiting area after his meeting with the chief pilot looking visibly shaken. With the unnerving realization of what was probably coming I asked, "Hey John, is this the big one?"

"Yeah," he answered solemnly, "this is the big one."

I walked the green mile to the chief pilot's office knowing full well that I was about to be let go but was totally unprepared for his convoluted verbal assault.

"It seems," he started out, "that on a recent trip to St. Croix, while you and the flight attendant were cleaning the airplane, you traded the bottle of rum that the FBO had given you as a gift to the flight attendant for the frozen steak that they had given her." He looked at me and continued, "We find that absolutely appalling. We are going to have to let you go."

Dumbfounded at the absurdity of what I had just heard, I could think of no proper response and simply said, "OK," and left the room. It wasn't until much later that I realized they were probably just trying to avoid having their unemployment taxes increased by "firing" us instead of laying us off. It is an improper and immoral tactic to be sure but not uncommon.

And so it was that just two short years into what I had considered the best job in the world, I found myself out of work with nothing more than a slightly fatter log book and a resume in need of an update.

The former abundance of flying positions available in Houston had dried up. In order to pay the bills I resorted to selling cars at a local dealership while trying to find another flying job.

What I had expected to be only a few weeks turned into a few months and it began to look like my unintentional career change might become permanent when I was given a new office mate at the dealership. He was a former air traffic controller who had also found himself in a career change resulting from the recent air traffic controllers' strike.

Bill, my office mate, didn't know exactly what he wanted to do career wise with his post ATC days, but knew I was still looking for a flying job. We were sitting in the office talking one day when I was paged for a phone call. As I reached to answer the phone, he placed his hand over mine preventing me from lifting the receiver. He looked at me and said, "If it's a guy named George from a map company, you called his secretary to schedule an interview about a flying job."

I took the call and wasn't all that surprised to hear, "Hi this is George. I'd like to meet for coffee and go over your resume."

After scheduling the meeting, I cradled the phone and looked at Bill. He simply said, "You're welcome."

"Bill," I said wavering between anger and thankfulness, "I don't want to fly some single engine airplane back and forth over the ground at five hundred feet making maps. What the hell were you thinking?"

"Oh just go on the interview," he said, "you never know."

George Parker did hire me but it wasn't to make maps. He had recently bought a small flight school that had a twin engine airplane and since we had hit if off during our visit, he wanted me to set up his charter department for him.

Working for George was a wonderful experience. He was a great boss and mentor. I learned a lot about business from him. He also didn't mind that I had higher aspirations and would let me take time off for the occasional airline interview when I could scare one up.

Besides sending resumes and filling out applications, my pursuit of an airline career also included reading trade publications. It was in one such publication that I began to follow the growth of the relatively new business of overnight packages.

Between Federal Express, Airborne, Emery and the relative new comer DHL, it was reported at the time that less than twenty percent of the potential market had been touched. Recognizing a potential growth area, I started applying to the freight carriers as well as the passenger carriers and then I got an idea.

It occurred to me that if there was a growing demand for time sensitive material in the overnight business it stood to reason that there may be a market for same day delivery of time sensitive material. Attorneys seemed to me to be the biggest users of time sensitive documents and there were thousands of them not only in Houston but also in the nearby cities of Dallas, Austin and San Antonio.

I pitched the idea of a flight service offering same day delivery of such documents to those cities and the boss liked it. We set up a flight schedule covering the four cities and I began beating the bushes promoting our new service to local businesses and law firms.

During one of my sales calls I bumped into Larry Miller who happened to be with DHL. He allowed that while they didn't have any need for our same day service, they did have a Lear Jet that would begin service to Dallas the following week and needed someone to provide an aircraft to fly a couple bags of material from Dallas to Houston each night.

We contracted with DHL and were the first to cover that route for them and were hoping it would lead to additional contracts on other routes. DHL was growing like a weed and I had envisioned dozens of aircraft flying routes for them all over the country.
George and I had discussed the idea of acquiring some larger aircraft for just that purpose and had even gone to Oklahoma to look at some Cessna 404s that had been parked by Emery when they opted for larger aircraft.

My vision was right. A couple of years later there were hundreds of aircraft flying routes for DHL all over the country but they were not ours. As it turned out, just a week after initiating the Dallas to Houston service for DHL I got a call from Larry Miller. He had cancelled our contract explaining that with DHL's tremendous growth there was too much material for the Lear Jet that had been servicing Dallas and that they were going to have to replace it as well.

In an effort to save our existing contract and the prospects for future contracts, I explained to Mr. Miller that we were able to put any size airplane on any route that he needed.

"No, no, no," he said, "we're going to ship everything as belly freight on common carriers. We're not going to be flying anything ourselves."

"I understand that you have several aircraft operating up and down the west coast. Surely you will need some additional lift in other parts of the country as you expand," I countered.

"Oh no," he told me again, "we're going to get rid of our own aircraft and stick with the idea of shipping everything on the scheduled carriers."

Knowing the growth that DHL and the industry as a whole was experiencing, I began to wonder if maybe I was dealing with the wrong guy and asked, "Who might I talk to in San Francisco that could point us in the right direction as to where you might need additional lift?"

He repeated his favorite phrase. "No, no, you would be wasting your time. They would tell you the same thing."

I recognized that I wasn't going to make any further progress with Mr. Miller but I knew where the industry was headed and fully intended to call San Francisco at some point. The distractions of day to day business kept me from making that call and it wasn't until years later that I would realize what could have been. Even though I didn't know it then, the small taste of ineptitude I experienced in my first dealings with DHL was indicative of a faulty corporate culture that permeated the company like a cancer.

Chapter Two

Pick Me, Pick Me

It is not uncommon for an airline to include a psychological evaluation in their interview process for pilot candidates. After all, no one wants to be on the flight where at thirty-five thousand feet the pilot all of a sudden decides he wants to meet Allah and fails to ask if everyone else wants to go with him before putting the airplane in a nose dive toward terra firma.

My faith in the interview process in general was somewhat shaken when just a few years after my interview with Delta Airlines I learned that the doctor with the rocking chair, the psychologist who was supposed to be weeding out those candidates with mental issues, had committed suicide. I never did find out if you were supposed to rock or not during the interview.

For the dedicated airline pilot wanna be, just getting called for an interview was quite an accomplishment. Efforts to gain the coveted invitation to an airline interview varied widely. Some subscribed to services that helped the prospective pilot develop a proper resume or to services that claimed to have the inside skinny on what a given airline might require as far as qualifications. Others took a more creative approach. There were stories of pilots enclosing their resumes in a shoe and sending it with a note saying they wanted to get a foot in the door. There was no end to the list of other such gimmicks.

It is my belief that such a tactic would have actually gotten my resume not only noticed but also thrown into the trash along with the now useless shoe. I kept my shoes on and continued filling out applications.

My flight time eventually built to the point that met the requirements of most airlines and when American Airlines called, I felt that I had a realistic shot. They provided a ticket to Dallas where the interview would be conducted and during the flight I mentally practiced answering questions that I thought were likely to be asked. What a waste of time that turned out to be. I'd have been better off worrying about how to explain that my grandfather had had a heart attack. Unbeknownst to me, the conventional wisdom about an interview with American at the time was that their intense focus on one's family medical history became a stumbling block to many otherwise suitable candidates.

Unlike my interview with Delta, the physical came first at American and it was a doozie. You would have thought these people were afraid the airplane would fall right out of the sky if the guy flying it for them didn't make an astronaut look like an unfit specimen. There have been earthlings abducted by aliens from space that haven't gone through such thorough probing.

I had just about recovered from the discomfort of the physical examination when they led us to the area for the hearing test. Nurse Ratched, the Nazi who was to administer the test, led me and a fellow interviewee to two side by side sound booths. Her gruff instructions were simply, "Put on the headset and push the button when you hear a beep."

As I sat down in the booth and started to adjust my headset, the burly nurse slammed the door shut like a prison guard trying to keep a fugitive from escaping. The booth had a viewing window on the side through which I could see a needle like writing mechanism which would be recording my responses. I could also see the booth to my left and its writing needle where the other pilot candidate was taking the test. Beeping and button pushing ensued but only for about thirty seconds. The sudden and surprising lack of any further beeping caused me to look out the little window at the other fellow's booth. His needle was still bouncing along indicating he still had an ample supply of beeps. My needle was just drawing a sickly little flat line. This test wasn't going well at all.

About the time it dawned on me that my machine had failed, nurse Ratched yanked the door open and growled, "Next stop, end of the hall." It must have been her intense concentration on the clipboard in her hand that left her totally oblivious to what I thought was a fairly obvious mechanical failure.

"Excuse me," I said, "my sound booth…."

She interrupted me in mid sentence, "I can't discuss the results with you."

"But the machine…..." I was again cut off.

"I can't discuss any results of the test."

Realizing that I was only going to be able to get a couple of words in before being cut off, I simply blurted out, "It's broken."

The Nazi nurse dramatically lowered the clipboard on which she had been concentrating and glared at me while repeating in a staccato cadence, "I cannot discuss the results of the test."

"Oh…so…down the… ah…hall here you say," I stammered as I made my retreat feeling fairly certain that my hearing test had been scored as a failure. Not that I got to discuss the results or anything.

Walking down the hall to the next stop I began to realize that the botched hearing test would almost certainly spell doom for any hopes that I may have had with American. At the end of the hall was the final step in the process. A young woman dressed like a nurse handed me an envelope and a card with three squares on it. I looked at it and back at her but before I could ask what it was, she explained that it was for me to take home and send them a stool sample.

Not having seen or heard of such a thing before, I offered it back to her and said, "Well it's certainly not going to fit in this envelope."

My attempt at lightheartedness was met with a sigh of exasperation and her explanation, "No, you use this stick and smear a small sample of your stool on the card each day for three days and then mail it back to us."

I walked away in disbelief thinking, "You've got to be kidding. These people actually want me to fish around in my toilet bowl and then of all things mail it to them."

Desperate people do desperate things to reach a goal and so it was that for three days I dutifully performed the undignified task that was asked of me. On the third day I sealed the envelope with a sponge because I didn't want to lick it and then I took it to the mail box but the mailman had already come. In the mail that day I had received a letter from American Airlines. The impersonal form letter thanked me for my interest and informed me that it regretted not being able to offer me employment with American Airlines.

Apparently they weren't as interested in my stool sample as they had led me to believe. Well, interested or not, they were going to get a sample and a good one. I retrieved my sample missive from the mail box and added a generous amount of "sample" the next day before mailing it. Not surprisingly, I never got to discuss the results of that test either.

There were other interviews but none of them included the undignified antics that I experienced at American. Republic called me for an interview but it was cancelled before I got to it due to their merger with North Western. A short time later I got a call from Eastern Airlines.

With a couple of interviews under my belt and the fair amount of flight time I had logged, I felt that the Eastern interview held great promise. My flight to Miami on the day of the interview deposited me at the last gate on one of the Eastern concourses. As I walked through the concourse to the main terminal area I could see the Eastern jets at their Jetways and could imagine myself one day flying one of them. There was the occasional flight crew walking to their flights and I could see myself in uniform walking to my flight. My confidence was growing with each step.

My interview at Eastern was the most pleasant I had ever experienced. Everyone was very friendly but still solidly professional. I was amazed at the tremendous sense of family and the powerful team spirit that was so evident. This was truly an airline that I wanted to fly for and a company that I wanted to be a part of.

The interview consisted of a physical and a visit with someone from the flight department. At the end of the process I met with a Human Resources rep who reviewed my paperwork, looked up at me with a smile and said, "Well, you've been selected to be in one of our upcoming new hire classes. They will call you in about two weeks with the class date."

Just as it was sinking in that I was actually going to be hired, I heard my name called. A nurse had popped her head in the door and said, "Mr. Turner we need you for just a minute. We would like to take a couple of x-rays before you leave."

During the x-rays I noticed that everyone else had already gone and it appeared that I had been singled out for the extra step. My assumption was that the lumbar laminectomy I had undergone just a couple years earlier had been the cause of the extra scrutiny.

About a week later the call came but it wasn't for a class date. Instead I was again thanked for my time and was told that they were sorry that they couldn't offer me employment at this time. There was no need for me to ask why there had been a change of plans. I was fairly sure it had been because of the back operation. They wouldn't have told me anyway. None of the airlines will tell you why you didn't get selected.

It was back to the drawing board for me. There was no time to worry about the one that got away. I did realize that the number of passenger carriers available to me was dwindling so I turned my attention to the overnight freight carriers. At that time UPS didn't have their own aircraft yet and you pretty much had to have a contact already working at Federal Express to get considered there.

A missionary had come to the church I was attending and during his slide presentation I noticed one of the slides showed a DHL canoe. The missionary explained that there was no mail where they were and that DHL was the only way they were able to get supplies and communications from home. I learned that this was the case in many parts of the world. With DHL covering the globe I began to imagine flying for them and being able to travel the world.

My friend Mike had recently been hired by DHL and I gave him a call. We met for dinner at a little seafood restaurant and while the dinner may not have been memorable, the meeting would be a turning point in my career.

It had been a couple years since I had set up the Dallas to Houston flight for DHL and they had grown so much that their Houston station was now being serviced with a Boeing 727. Mike was very enthusiastic about DHL's growth and their plans for the future. He explained that their fleet consisted of ten twin engine turboprops, a couple of Lear Jets and three Boeing 727s with more on the way. I asked Mike to get me an application.

I was very pleasantly surprised when just a couple weeks after sending in the application Mike had given me, I got a phone call from Ed Byrd of DHL's human resources department. After the obligatory social niceties Mr. Byrd said, "Well I have looked over your application and I see that you are a Captain on the Lear Jet and the King Air 200. We are only hiring First Officers. I doubt if you would want to take a lesser position."

"I wouldn't expect to start out as a Captain," I assured him. "That would be the case at any airline."

"Well, you know our starting pay is not that much. If you came to work here you would be making a lot less than what you are used to," he countered.

"Starting pay is always a bit lower with a new position and it would be worth a cut in pay to have a schedule instead of being on call all the time," I said.

It was almost as if he was trying to discourage me as he continued, "But you have been flying jets and here you would initially be on the turboprop."

"Yes sir, I understand that. I think it would be a good career step for me," I said sensing that he was trying to see if I really wanted to work specifically for DHL. I must have convinced him that I did because the conversation ended successfully with an invitation to Cincinnati for an interview.

A couple weeks later I arrived at DHL's hub in Cincinnati for my interview with the Chief Pilot and was directed to some offices on the second floor. A young lady from human resources met me and said, "I'm sorry the Chief Pilot was called out of town but you can sit here at this desk and fill out your new hire paper work. Welcome to DHL."

Of course there was a physical and a sim check that I needed to pass but as it turned out, my phone conversation with Ed Byrd was my interview. That unconventional encounter was the first of many I would experience with DHL over the next twenty-four years.

Chapter Three

Living the Dream

Over the course of the last few years as I had been interviewing with various airlines, I had grown accustom to seeing the well designed training facilities and had pictured myself starting my career in such a setting. That was not the case at DHL. At other airlines, when you did a sim check (an opportunity for the prospective employer to see something of how you fly) it was done in a really for real simulator. Our sim check at DHL was done with a table top model that was really just a PC with a toy type control yoke. It didn't really matter if it was a full blown simulator or not as long as they liked what they saw, which they did and so when all was said and done there were ten of us selected for the new hire class. Our initial ground school training was conducted in the DHL training facility which consisted of a double wide trailer parked on the ramp beside the sort center. I really shouldn't have been surprised after seeing the "simulator" but I was willing to cut them some slack since they were a relatively new company and surely would improve as they grew. After all, I had reached a career goal. I was with an airline and things could only get better, right?

The statistical average failure rate during initial training among new hires throughout the airline industry was about twenty percent. Our class was statistically average in that we lost two of the original ten class members but not due to an inability to perform. It turned out that some of the flight time one of our guys had logged was actually dump truck driving time and he was invited to leave for lying on his application. One other class mate quit in a huff after being assigned a seniority number that put him at the bottom of the list. Industry standard protocol is that the oldest in a new hire class be given the top seniority number and so on down to the youngest, which he was. Technically speaking, while the entire industry called it a Seniority List, to DHL that smacked of union affiliation and so they called it a Flight Crew List. This reinvention of the wheel on the part of DHL was the first of many I would experience. Either way, Darwin's Theory of Natural Selection had rid our herd of those that were unworthy, and the eight of us that remained all made it through training.

The initial assignment for a new hire at DHL was to the right seat of the Swearingen SW-4 Metroliner which was a stretched version of the Merlin twin engine turboprop. A right seater is called a First Officer which is a copilot. After a period of time and when the position becomes available a First Officer can upgrade to the left seat as a Captain.

There is a tremendous amount of cost involved with training flight crews. In most cases they are getting paid while in training but aren't really productive since they are not out flying revenue flights. There is also a combination of various other costs which can include things like hotels, per diem or travel expenses and even fuel and maintenance costs for those times when training might be conducted in an aircraft as opposed to a simulator. In most cases a new hire pilot would be trained as a

First Officer and when the time came for them to upgrade they would be taken off line and would go through training again as a Captain. When a pilot would finish ground school and simulator training and was ready to fly the line they would spend the first few days or so flying with a Check Airman who would help them put what they had learned into practice then sign them off. This process was known as Initial Operating Experience or IOE. IOE was required anytime a pilot was assigned a new position or aircraft type.

DHL was experiencing very rapid growth and pilots were upgrading to Captain very quickly. In a move designed to reduce training costs and streamline the process DHL decided to train the new hire pilots as Captains right from the start by giving them a type rating in the airplane during their initial training. A type rating is an authorization to fly a specific aircraft type and is listed on your pilot license. It is required for aircraft that weigh over 12,500 pounds or are powered by jet engines. Because there are some additional training steps and a more extensive check ride, type ratings are usually not given to those being trained as First Officers.

Those of us in my new hire class would be the first to benefit from this new plan. We would be typed and go fly the line as First Officers and when we would be eligible to upgrade to Captain all we would have to do is complete our Captain IOE. It was a great plan and should have worked well but nothing is ever simple.

My new hire class started in August 1986. I finished training, got my type rating in the Metroliner and started flying the line as a First Officer in early October 1986. It was just a couple months later in mid December when I was told that

I would upgrade to Captain the following week. I was scheduled to operate the Kansas City flight inbound as a First Officer and on the next outbound flight I would start my IOE. An upgrade to Captain meant two things that every pilot likes: another stripe and more pay.

Our Kansas City layover hotel was the one that several years earlier had experienced the collapse of an elevated walkway in its lobby. The tragedy was understandably not noted anywhere in the lobby and of course everything looked normal but knowing that it had happened felt odd. I remember wondering if the desk clerks had to put up with many questions about it and decided I wouldn't add to their discomfort by mentioning it.

As the Captain and I were checking out of our rooms in preparation for that evening's flight back to Cincinnati the desk clerk handed us a note from DHL. Gandy, the newly appointed Assistant Flight Manager wanted me to call him before we went to the airport. The desk clerk directed me to a bank of pay phones around the corner from the front desk.

Gandy's halting demeanor and the nerves evident in his voice indicated a problem greater than his explanation allowed as he said, "I know we had planned for you to start your Captain IOE on your outbound flight tonight but we aren't going to be able to do that."

"Well, that's OK Gandy," I said. "If there's not a slot available right now, I can wait until they have one."

"No, that's not it," he continued. "There's a problem."

"Oh, well what is it? I'm sure we can get it worked out when I get in," I offered, thinking there must be some sort of administrative detail that still needed finalized.

"I can't tell you," he allowed.

"OK, I'm a little confused now. You say there is a problem but you can't tell me what it is?"

"Yes, it's a disciplinary situation but I can't discuss it with you."

"Then why did you have me call you?" I asked.

"Well, to let you know that you won't be upgrading yet. We'll talk more when you get in."

Of course common sense would dictate that bad news should always wait instead of being offered right before the recipient has a critical task to perform. Though the confusing situation was weighing on my mind, as a professional I tried not to let it affect my performance on the flight to Cincinnati. After landing I met with Gandy only to learn that the situation had gotten completely out of hand. I couldn't tell if it was a case of ineptitude on Gandy's part as a new Assistant Flight Manager or if he was just passing along what had been given to him by Bam Bam, the new Flight Manager who had appointed Gandy.

I eventually learned that a Captain I had previously flown with had complained about my performance. When I explained that since I had not had any problems with nor any complaints from any of the Captains I had flown with, perhaps the complaint had to do with another First Officer and not myself. Gandy assured me that it was indeed about me and explained that they had recently started asking Captains for performance reports on First Officers in order to evaluate those that were close to upgrading.

When I asked what it was that I was reported to have done wrong, Gandy again told me that he couldn't discuss it. I was dumbfounded. Thinking that I couldn't have possibly heard him properly I said again with the gentlest voice I could muster under the circumstances, "I've completed all of the training and met all of the requirements to upgrade to Captain. If you would just let me know what it is that I am reported to have done I am sure there is a normal explanation that can put all of this behind us."

Gandy once again illogically explained that it couldn't be discussed and told me that what they had decided was to send me home on paid administrative time off while they worked out a solution. After noticing the astonished look of disbelief on my face, he told me that I could call Bam Bam the next day to learn more.

I drove home in total confusion. This was supposed to be my dream airline job. My career goals were finally met and now this nightmare was happening. I had no idea what I could have possibly done wrong. None of the Captains had any complaints at all. What kind of crazy people had I gotten mixed up with? Was this the kind of thing that I could look forward to for the rest of my time with this company?

The next day I would call Bam Bam. Bam Bam was one of those guys that always had to be running something or be in charge of something. He fancied himself a great, deep thinking leader of men. After a stint as Flight Manager he took a position as Manager of Flight Training and later moved into some other upper middle management position. He told stories of his heroism during the Viet Nam war and claimed to have been awarded the Medal of Honor. As a manager he fought against unionization when the pilot group started organizing but after leaving the management fold he ran for and was elected as president of our local union council touting his desire and ability to help us all get more out of our careers at DHL.

It was later learned that he hadn't actually been given the medal he claimed to have been awarded and was fired for lying on his application. The reports were that he then went to work for the Teamsters which was the union that represented the pilot group at ABX Air, the very group that was a part of the chaos that led to the eventual shut down of our airline.

Of course I didn't know any of that then nor did I know he had an extremely heavy handed management style until my uncomfortable phone conversation with him.

After a couple deep breaths I worked up the nerve to call and explained to him that I had no idea what was supposed to have happened since Gandy said he couldn't discuss any of the details with me. He said, "The other day you flew with Red and he said you didn't know how much fuel was on the airplane."

I recalled the flight he had referenced and began to feel some relief knowing that there had simply been a misunderstanding. "Oh, OK, now I understand what must have happened." I started, "This can be easily cleared up….."

Bam Bam interrupted me in mid sentence with an unnecessarily harsh rebuke saying, "Now watch what you say and watch how you say it. What you say now can determine how far you will go with DHL." The tone and tenor of his forceful rant left no doubt that the rest of the conversation would be one sided and I would have no further input. I was to stay at home until they decided what to do with me.

I seriously considered leaving the company but thought, "No, I'm not letting them take this away from me." Fortunately a few weeks later I was able to finish my IOE and upgrade to Captain. The emotional upheaval and stomach convulsions stemming from a situation over which I had no control but which almost caused me to leave what ultimately was a good career position would unfortunately be revisited several times throughout my tenure at DHL.

OK, since you asked, I'll tell you what actually happened. The Metroliner was a relatively small aircraft. It's appearance reminded one of a cardboard tube like the inside of a paper towel roll but with a tail and wings. It was not necessarily an attractive aircraft to my mind and most of us called it "The Manned Weather Probe." Because the fuselage was narrow, it couldn't hold much bulk and so the gross weight of the freight was never a factor that affected the fuel load. Consequently our procedures required that all the Metros be fueled to the same level before each outbound flight.

It was the First Officer's duty to go out and perform a preflight inspection of the aircraft and that included verifying that it had been fueled to the required, standard amount. The preflight was to be accomplished one half hour before flight time.

On the night that I was reported to have committed the heinous act, I was standing outside the pilot room watching the machines of the sort facility when Red, the Captain on the flight came up to me and asked, "How much fuel is on the airplane?"

As a Captain on the aircraft Red would have been expected to be familiar with the company procedures used in preflighting and operating the aircraft. That meant he would know what the standard fuel load would be so I had to assume that his question was really meant to find out if I had done the preflight yet. It was a little more than an hour before our scheduled departure and I hadn't been to the airplane yet so I said to him, "It should be at the standard level but I can go out and do the preflight early if you would like."

"Well...well...," he stammered, "we leave in about an hour."

"No problem," I said, "I'll go out now." I headed out to the airplane wondering if he was confused as to when the preflight was required to be done. A competent Captain would discuss any areas of concern with his crew but I never heard anything more from Red and had no reason to think there was a problem. Red's lack of familiarity with standard operating procedures and inability to properly relate to another crew member led to the filing of his fallacious report which caused the violent overreaction by management.

Such was my baptism into a corporate culture that was the very incarnation of a "shoot then yell freeze" mentality. It is interesting to note that Red was later found to be deficient in judgement after a few actual misdeeds on his part. During a flight I was on with him from Cincinnati to Lincoln, Nebraska we experienced a depressurization at FL240 which is twenty-four thousand feet. He declared an emergency and we donned our oxygen masks and descended to 10,000 feet. After we leveled off, the pressurization system appeared to be working again and Red requested a climb back to our original altitude. I told him I wasn't comfortable with the climb since we were unable to determine what had caused the loss of pressurization but he wanted to climb back up to altitude. He was later counseled for his decision which had been noted by management as they reviewed his report of the incident.

Several years later after we had gained representation by ALPA (The Air Line Pilot's Association) Red had failed to show for an assignment and was fired. The union helped him get his job back but he repeated the same infraction three more times. The union helped him get his job back in all but the last iteration and he found himself unemployed in an example of what I suppose could be called airline Karma.

I flew as Captain on the Metroliner for the next year or so. While I enjoyed my time in the turboprop I really was looking forward to getting into the Boeing. The 727 was one of the airplanes I dreamed about flying as far back as my days in high school. There were times when I would play hooky from school and drive to the airport just to sit on the observation deck and watch the jets. The sleek shape of the Boeing 727 was a thing of beauty. It just looked like what you would expect an airplane to look like.

Chapter Four

If It's Not Boeing, I'm Not Going

I happened to catch a news report recently about the last scheduled flight operation of the 727 at Fed Ex and it felt like a small part of me died. It didn't seem like it was that long ago I had read that the last new 727 to be built had come off of the production line at the Boeing plant and was delivered to Fed Ex. The 727 has provided lift for most of the world's air carriers and will always be considered one of the most iconic aircraft ever flown.

Today's airline fleet is mostly comprised of modern aircraft designed to be operated by a two person crew which would be the Captain and the First Officer. In the "olden" days when I was starting my aviation career the standard transport category aircraft required three crew members. In addition to the Captain and First Officer there was a Flight Engineer whose job in the cockpit was to manage the fuel, hydraulic, electric and pressurization systems along with a few other non flying tasks.

A separate license is required to be a Flight Engineer and one can be an FE without being a pilot. There were some airlines that had what they termed PFE's which was a Professional Flight Engineer who didn't fly but remained in the engineer seat for their career. For the most part though, airlines hired pilots into the engineer seat and then moved them up to First Officer and eventually Captain. The Flight Engineer license, like most licenses issued by the FAA required a written test and a check ride. Once the written test was passed, the results were good for two years. After that, if a check ride hadn't been passed and a license issued, the written test would need to be retaken.

In that era, most airlines required the prospective pilot to have their FE written test passed to be considered for employment. The good news was that if you were employed by an airline that operated under FAR Part 121, (the part of the Federal Aviation Regulations that govern scheduled air carriers) your FE written test results would be good indefinitely.

I had been flying the Metroliner for DHL for about a year and a half when they posted the availability of a few Flight Engineer positions on the Boeing 727. My bid for one of the positions was successful and brought me that much closer to fulfilling a life long dream of being a crew member on a large jet airliner. It is aviation's version of the "Big Dance" as they call it in baseball and I had been called up from the minors.

Most people would think of school as being a boring pain in the neck but we got to talk aircraft systems and procedures all day. This was exciting stuff. After systems we spent a week practicing checklist usage, procedures and crew coordination in the PTM, the Procedural Trainer Mockup which we called the paper tiger. It was really nothing more than pictures of the cockpit arranged in the shape of the cockpit on a metal frame with three chairs that we sat in to simulate being in the aircraft. While it doesn't sound like much, you have to remember that we were getting paid to play like we were flying a 727. That's a pretty good gig in my book.

The next phase was the actual simulator. Oh baby! I have always said that if it wasn't for the fact that you had to pass a check ride to keep your job, flying a simulator is the best video game in the world.

At the time I moved into the back seat of the 727 as a Flight Engineer, DHL didn't have their own simulator so we rented sim time from U.S. Air and used their training facility in Pittsburg. For dinner and drinks, some of our down time was spent in a little eatery called Wings, Spuds and Suds which was near the training center and the hotel where we stayed. As the name would suggest, the pub type restaurant specialized in beer, fries and Buffalo Wings offered in various flavors and levels of garlic. Prevailing wisdom suggested that to be the only one in the sim that had not enjoyed wings the night before was to suffer greatly.

Most of the time in the sim is spent dealing with various emergency situations that you may experience in the real aircraft. It may have been a grueling grind to constantly practice emergency after emergency but when one popped up in real life it was sure nice to see your training take over resulting in a safe and successful outcome.

With sim and IOE completed I was flying the line as a Flight Engineer in a Boeing 727 jetliner for a Part 121 carrier. The years of preparation had paid off. While I did look forward to the day I could upgrade to First Officer and eventually Captain, I wanted to enjoy my time in the back seat and I did for the most part.

One of the things that any pilot flying in a crew situation is aware of is Cockpit Resource Management. CRM as it is known, is the process of managing the flight crew using proper coordination and communication to produce a safe and efficient flight operation. During the early weeks of my time as a Flight Engineer I found myself flying with a Captain named Grim Blisskill. Grim was a good stick meaning he could physically fly the airplane very well. His CRM however, left a lot to be desired. He probably would have made a better fighter pilot than airline Captain. Grim had tremendous head knowledge but would use it to club other crew members as opposed to guiding them. His rebukes were sharp and given with an attitude that belittled those on the receiving end. He could make life miserable in the cockpit. The result was that he created an atmosphere that was brittle and tended to cause some crew members to effectively pull back from full participation.

On one flight with Grim going into San Francisco we had been handed off to the tower by approach control. The First Officer was working the radios as Grim flew the approach. It was one of those beautiful, clear sunny mornings with smooth air and Grim made a nice landing. As he finished the landing roll and turned onto the taxiway the First Officer called the tower and told them we were clearing the active runway and requested taxi to the DHL ramp. The tower controller answered, "Roger DHL 104. You are cleared to land. Taxi to the ramp."

All three of us realized at that moment that we had failed to call the tower to get landing clearance. While the controller was gracious enough to say we were cleared to land and get it on the tape without giving us any grief we knew we were lucky to have gotten away with one. While we had been flying all night and fatigue played a big part in our misstep to be sure, all of us were at fault and I often wondered if a more relaxed cockpit with better CRM could have made a difference.

Speed, power and other settings are calculated taking into account the aircraft weight, outside air temperature, airport elevation and runway length when planning a take off or landing. Along with operating the various aircraft systems, these calculations are a part of the Flight Engineer's job. The engineer would look up the numbers and then hand the "TOLD" cards to the flying pilots. Our TOLD (take off and landing data) cards at the time were in the form of a set of laminated flip cards with speed and flap settings on them. When not being used, the TOLD flip cards were stored in a desk at the engineer's position that had a table top which opened up to access a small storage area.

After a long week I was looking forward to the end of my series of flights with Grim. It had been a very difficult week of walking on egg shells half of the time and sitting on pins and needles the rest of the time. He pretty much sucked the fun right out of flying and I didn't think that was even possible. At least our layover was in Miami which I hoped would offer a bit of relaxation even though it was only for the day. We landed, taxied to parking and accomplished the parking checklist. Grim handed me the TOLD cards and I put them in my desk.

I slept all day then had dinner at a little place next to the hotel that served a wonderful linguini with white clam sauce. After that it was time to put on the uniform and catch the crew van to the airport.

My exterior preflight and walk around were complete and we were all three in the cockpit waiting for the weight and balance paperwork to show up so we could figure our takeoff performance numbers. When we finished that, Grim asked for the TOLD cards but I couldn't find them. Grim seemed unusually irritated and started a rant about there being a place for things and berating me for not having put them in their place. I was told that we were likely to be late and it would be my fault because I had lost valuable equipment that I should have taken better care of. We finally found out that the mechanics had taken them out of the desk for some reason and had them in their office. They brought them out to us and the flight continued to Cincinnati on time and without incident.

The landing in Cincinnati was uneventful but that didn't mean everything was fine. After the parking checklist we were closing up our flight bags and getting ready to leave the airplane. The First Officer was already outside but stuck his head back in the cockpit to tell us the crew van was there. I picked up my bag and was starting to leave the cockpit and Grim said, "You can't go to the crew van yet. You haven't done your post flight walk around."

I stupidly said, "What do you mean?"

Grim told the First Officer to go ahead and take the crew van in and we would call for another one when we were ready. He then said to me, "Why didn't you do a post flight inspection like the manual requires?"

Having recently just finished training, I was fairly up to speed on what was expected of me and I pride myself on being the kind of professional that tries to learn the job properly but for the life of me,

I couldn't remember ever having been instructed to do a post flight walk around. I didn't believe it was listed in our operations manual but I was new and didn't want to say, "It's not in the book," and later be shown to be wrong so I simply said, "I don't remember reading that it needed to be done."

"Go out and do your walk around," Grim said, "then come back up here and see me."

After looking over the airplane to make sure nothing had fallen off during the flight, I went back up to the cockpit. Grim had me sit in the Flight Engineer's seat while he sat in the Captain's seat twisting around to face me for his speech. Over the next fifteen minutes I was forced to sit and listen to how I was no good and would never amount to anything at DHL or any other airline and would probably be fired. He expressed his surprise that I had been hired in the first place. That familiar feeling in the pit of my stomach resulting from other unnecessary psychological beatings was there and I couldn't help but think, "It's happening again."

When he was done I walked to the hub building not wanting to ride with Grim on the crew van. Once I was inside, the first thing I did was comb through the operations manual to see if a post flight inspection was required. I was relieved and not completely surprised to learn that there was no such requirement. It was reassuring to know that I hadn't done anything contrary to required procedures in case the situation was brought to the attention of management as I fully expected it to be.

A couple days went by without my being called into the Flight Manager's office and I wondered how I had escaped another suspension or worse until I checked my mail file and saw the answer. In everyone's mail file there was a revision to the operations manual that now required a post flight inspection. My guess is that Grim went to them about our flight and it was discovered that something that should have been in the books had been omitted.

I promised myself that I would never again fly with Grim. A person's career could be jeopardized by his maniacal ravings even if that person wasn't at fault. I didn't care if I had to use sick days, vacation days or trade trips with someone. It wasn't worth my career or sanity to put up with such lunacy. I was able to avoid flying with Grim for the rest of my time at DHL, but the airline was small enough he couldn't be avoided all together and he would later go about wreaking havoc in areas other than just the cockpit.

Chapter Five

We're Moving On Up

Upgrades can come at a painfully slow pace if an airline isn't experiencing any growth. During the late seventies and early eighties there were times when the growth rate was at a standstill industry wide. TWA was reported to have Flight Engineers that had been in the engineer seat for seventeen or eighteen years without a chance to upgrade to a flying seat.

As aircraft systems got more sophisticated it began to make sense for manufacturers to start building aircraft that could be handled by a two person crew negating the need for a Flight Engineer. Airbus had originally designed the A-300 for a two person crew but the airlines weren't very receptive to the idea initially so Airbus put in an engineer seat and didn't go back to the two person concept until a few years later. One early entrant into the two person crew concept that did gain acceptance was the Boeing 737 which is still very popular.

Not everyone was thrilled with the idea of reducing the crew compliment by a third. Pilot groups felt that one less person in the cockpit per airplane meant less seniority for veteran crew members and less opportunity for potential new hires. United's pilots were able to get it in their contract that the 737 would have an engineer seat and Boeing put one in the 737s they delivered to United.

Since the systems would pretty much take care of themselves in a 737 it is hard to imagine what there was for a Flight Engineer to do other than read the checklists and maybe set the power. I was between flights in the Cleveland Hopkins Airport terminal having a cup of coffee once and struck up a conversation with a United pilot. He said he was a Flight Engineer on the 737 and had been for fifteen years. When I asked him if that was boring he said, "Oh no, I love it. It's the best job in the world."

It was encouraging to know that the work I loved could be enjoyable for years to come but it's still the case that all pilots want to upgrade at some point. That wasn't a problem at DHL. The company was growing rapidly and I spent only one year in the engineer seat before I got the chance to check out as a First Officer which was considered to be the best job on the property since the Flight Engineer did all the work and the Captain had all the responsibility. There was probably no other airline in the world at that time where upgrades came so quickly.

Training was still being done at the U.S. Air facility then, which was a very nice facility and provided a comfortable training environment. Throughout airline history it had been the case that if one had spent too much time in the back seat, their flying skills would get rusty but since it had only been a year for me I felt it wouldn't prove to be a problem. My relief at not having to shake off too much rust was short lived and an extra amount of pressure was heaped back onto my shoulders when I learned that my instructor for the upgrade training would be Grim. While I had successfully avoided flying with him since his verbal assault almost a year earlier, this wasn't something I could do anything about. I was going to have to suck it up, be professional and find some way to get through it.

I was pleasantly surprised to find that Grim wasn't as difficult to deal with in the sim as he was in the real airplane and I was able to find value in his "by the book" approach when it wasn't being administered with verbal abuse. His delivery may have been forceful and stern but at least it was tolerable during training.

Simulator time is extremely valuable since there is so much that needs to be crammed into each session to properly prepare for the check ride. That's why, given his normally unyielding, strict, no nonsense attitude, it was so surprising that Grim was a no-show for one of the sim sessions. Typically the crew of trainees would wait in the coffee lounge area of the training facility for the instructors to meet us and we would all head to the simulator but that day it was over a half hour into what was to be our sim time and no Grim. The Flight Engineer candidate and his instructor and the other pilot candidate and I were about ready to call it a day when we saw Grim heading toward us from the direction of the simulators with a female companion. Here this straight laced, by the book guy had used our sim time to give the young lady a tour of the simulator. We smiled to ourselves recognizing his actions to be something the Discovery Channel would call a display of feathers by the male of the species.

I survived training and would enjoy flying as First Officer for the next five years as I looked forward to making Captain and reaching the pinnacle of my aviation career. Some pilots never have the chance to make Captain during their career. For there to be upgrade opportunities an airline has to be growing by adding aircraft and routes. You've heard me say it before but being at the right place at the right time can pay off handsomely as it did for me having been hired at the beginning of DHL's tremendous growth phase.

In fact DHL's business was growing so fast they had to add additional lift beyond what they were able to fly themselves. It got to where the ramp was covered with so many 727s, Convairs and other assorted aircraft from charter operators that they outnumbered our own fleet by quite a bit. It was disheartening to show up for work and see ten or twelve jets from other carriers and only four or five DHL aircraft on the ramp. The pilot group wasn't pleased to see other carriers doing what should have been our flying and we constantly encouraged DHL to acquire additional aircraft. We pointed out to DHL management that they would save money flying their freight themselves instead of providing a profit to the other carriers but our encouragement seemed to fall on deaf ears.

DHL would occasionally add an airplane to the fleet but they were too cheap to do it properly. They found one old 727 in the jungles of South or Central America somewhere and paid something like three hundred thousand dollars for it thinking they had saved a million dollars or so compared to a normally priced 727. They ended up spending over a million and a half getting it into flying condition. One would have thought that with their penchant for saving money, DHL would have jumped at the idea of replacing charter aircraft with their own. Instead, they hired a consulting firm at a cost of several hundred thousand dollars only to be told what the pilot group had been telling them all along, "Get your own airplanes."

At least they listened to their consultants and went out and found several 727s to add to the fleet. They also added a new aircraft type which was the DC-8. It was a four engine jet that was a generation older than the Boeing 727 and also past it's prime days as a passenger jet but had become a favorite work horse in the freight industry. It had a lot more range than the 727 and carried twice the freight which made it attractive for some of the longer international routes that DHL had been chartering out to other carriers.

It is industry standard that the pay is greater on larger aircraft so a DC-8 pilot would make more than his counterpart on the 727. Even with the increase in pay, I never really wanted to fly the DC-8. While I liked the idea of international flying, we did enough of that on the 727 for my taste. For some reason I was never really attracted to the DC-8. Sure it looked OK and all but it just wasn't my cup of tea. Besides, Grim had transitioned to the eight and it would be a lot easier to avoid flying with him if I stayed in the seven two.

With the additional aircraft in the fleet, my chance for a Captain upgrade had arrived. By this time DHL had its own training center and simulator so training was done in Cincinnati near our hub at the airport. My time and experience in the airplane over the last few years made ground school a little easier and more enjoyable than it was when just starting out and I was looking forward to the sim.

I got Ted for an instructor in the sim. Ted is one of those guys that is just plain fun and he made learning fun. He was also a bit mischievous as I would later discover. We were about half way through sim training and I asked Ted if it would be OK if my girlfriend watched one of the sessions. He welcomed her into the sim the next day and made her feel at home.

A typical sim session consists of the Captain candidate and the First Officer candidate taking turns practicing the maneuvers scheduled for that session. I went first that day. We were working on engine out procedures such as engine failures and engine fires. It's interesting to note that there has never been a dual engine failure in a 727 except for once in a war zone and on that occasion the failures were due to damage from munitions fire. Even so, for Captain training we were required to demonstrate the ability to handle a dual engine failure to receive our type rating.

I finished my half of the training and the First Officer repeated the emergencies we were practicing as the flying pilot. The non-flying pilot (me in this case) would work the radios and coordinate the checklists with the Flight Engineer. When both pilots were done with their work in the sim we would usually hear the instructor say, "OK, let's go debrief." But that day after the First Officer was done Ted said, "OK Kim, it's your airplane. I have you lined up on the runway for take off."

Having already done what I knew was scheduled for the day's session I began to wonder if maybe I hadn't performed properly and needed to repeat a maneuver. There was little time to wonder. It could be sorted out later, but right now I had to make a takeoff. "I got the airplane," I said as I took the controls and called for the before takeoff checklist.

It was the simulator after all so I fully expected an engine failure at V1, the most critical time that you can lose one, and I wasn't disappointed. At 400 feet above the ground I called for the engine failure checklist and had the First Officer declare an emergency and request a turn back to the airport. As he was picking up his microphone to make the call, another engine failed and we were down to just one engine running.

"This is really tournament level stuff," I thought to myself. We had already done a dual engine failure and I began to wonder what was happening. My thoughts were interrupted by the Flight Engineer's voice.

"We have a failure in the B hydraulic system," he reported.

"Work with the First Officer and clean up what you can," I yelled over my shoulder as I fought the controls. "I'm going to try to keep this thing in the air long enough to make it back to the airport."

As I turned my base leg leaving only one more turn to line up with the runway I heard the fire bell sound. "What's on fire now?" I asked. This was now well beyond even tournament level. After all, we weren't supposed to be given multiple emergencies during the course of normal training.

"APU fire," the engineer called out.

"Silence the bell," I said not wanting to take the time to call for the entire checklist when we were so close to the ground. I turned final and lined up with the runway then called for the final flap setting for landing only to hear the First Officer tell me they had failed in position and wouldn't extend.

We were losing altitude faster than would have made for a proper glide slope and I called for max thrust on the remaining engine. As the First Officer pushed the thrust lever full forward, the last engine quit on us.

There wasn't enough altitude left to glide to the runway and we knew we were going to land short but could do nothing but watch the ground come up to meet us. After the impact we turned around to find out what was going on only to see Ted and my girlfriend laughing their asses off.

It turned out that after our training was done, Ted had turned to my girlfriend and said, "Kim passed his training. Would you like to see him crash?"

A lot had happened in the nineties both for DHL and for me. The old original class rooms on wheels were gone and where they used to sit was a new extension of the hub facility that was about four times the size of what was there when I got hired. It was about then that we started hearing rumors about DHL buying Airborne Express.

Chapter Six

The Beatings Will Continue Until Morale Improves

The new hub building was quite a step up from the old facility. It had room for a cafeteria, classrooms, a bigger pilot lounge and more offices. We needed more offices since the growth of the airline required additional managers. Now along with the System Chief Pilot, we also had a 727 Chief Pilot and a DC-8 Chief Pilot. As if the pilot group didn't have enough problems, Grim had managed to weasel his way into the position of System Chief Pilot and that made him dangerous to a greater number of careers than before when he was just in the cockpit.

Grim wasn't the only land mine you had to avoid stepping on during your career at DHL. Since we were a young carrier there were times when we had to bring in some expertise, such as an experienced instructor, from the outside. They were usually typed in the airplane they taught and would occasionally fly as Captain out of seniority (others that were hired before them hadn't upgraded yet) to stay current on what they were teaching. Most of the guys could accept that as a necessary part of what had to be done. What the pilot group as a whole didn't like was a junior guy gaming the system in order to get typed and or fly as Captain out of seniority.

Such was the case with Pumpkin Head. We called him that because of the gigantic, bulbous appendage on his shoulders. He was a bit short and when he climbed into and out of the humongous truck he drove to work he resembled Yosemite Sam.

Somehow even with so little jet time that he wasn't even qualified to fly as Captain on the Boeing, he was able to obtain an appointment as the 727 Chief Pilot. The pilot group, feeling wronged by his promotion, joined together in a display of solidarity that expressed itself in the form of Halloween pumpkin stickers. Every cubby hole, table top or access panel in every airplane was plastered with pumpkin stickers. Throughout the entire DHL system, every office and crew room had pumpkin stickers on the walls. Pumpkin Head remained oblivious to the fact that he was being ridiculed on such a major scale for several months. By the time he caught on to what was happening, the situation had gotten so out of hand that the company had to have the union ask the pilots to stop putting pumpkin stickers everywhere. It didn't help his cause any when shortly after the "Great Sticker Prohibition" Pumpkin Head tried unsuccessfully to dye his hair turning it orange. Lacking the foresight to attempt to dye it back to its original color, he actually showed up for work like that and got irritated at the constant snickering.

Managers often feel the need to justify their existence by finding something to manage. I believe that may have been the impetus behind a summons to Pumpkin Head's office that I received. When I arrived he was looking at a computer print out and told me that I held the record for taking more sick days than anyone else in the pilot group.

Pumpkin Head's voice made him sound like Mickey Mouse and it was sometimes difficult to take him seriously. I actually thought he was joking and said, "Is there a prize for that?" He didn't think that was funny but didn't make too much out of it due to embarrassment once I explained that the total time I had taken off as shown in his print out was comprised of vacation days, and pre-approved holidays as well as sick days. I don't know what had possessed him to select me for scrutinization but suffice it to say, he would bear watching.

Noise had become a hot button issue at many airports and those of us in the aviation business were tasked with being "good neighbors" to those living in communities that were near the airports out of which we operated. Being a good neighbor generally involved what is called "noise abatement procedures" which is another way of saying fly your airplane using altitudes, headings and power settings that you normally wouldn't use so that you make less noise around a community that has complained a lot. I still don't understand how trains seem to have escaped the ire of the noise sensitive complainants that have plagued aviation so tirelessly.

Several airports had noise curfews that restricted flight operations. Landings and takeoffs were limited by time of day and the type of aircraft that was being operated. Infractions of these restrictions could mean hefty fines for air carriers.

Shortly after my upgrade to Captain I witnessed these noise curfews along with flawed managers and maintenance problems combine with weather to create the most iconic display of stupidity and ineptitude I had ever experienced. It was a three day fiasco of Keystone Cop like buffoonery rife with the type of self serving misdirection normally employed by corrupt politicians in an attempt to divert attention from their own misdeeds and place the blame on others.

There was a gigantic, late season snow storm moving across the country and about to hit Cincinnati before it moved on to the Eastern seaboard. I was scheduled for the trip that stops in Boston then Bradley and returns to Cincinnati through Boston the next evening. Boston had a noise curfew and Gene, one of the Flight Mangers had put out a memo concerning the noise curfew at Boston and warning that the State of Massachusetts would prosecute the individual pilot as well as fine the company for violating the curfew.

We were scheduled to takeoff for Boston at 6:00 AM and the storm was already dumping snow on the ground at Cincinnati and would hit the East coast sometime that evening and could cause delays system wide. The aircraft we were scheduled to take on the Boston trip was a Stage II aircraft which meant that per the curfew, it couldn't take off after 10PM. I went to Ryan, the Flight Manager on duty that morning and suggested that we should consider changing to an aircraft that would meet the noise restrictions. My reasoning was that if there were to be a delay on our outbound leg from Bradley because of the weather coming through, we would then be late for our subsequent Boston departure and would violate the curfew.

There was a spare aircraft available that met the needed criteria and a possible fine or service interruption could have easily been avoided. Instead, Ryan's reaction to my attempt at preventing a future problem was one of total disinterest. I don't know if he just didn't care or if the idea didn't appeal to him because he didn't come up with it himself. Even after our aircraft had a mechanical issue Ryan failed to allow the swap so the spare aircraft went unused and we suffered a delay.

Heavy snow was falling so we got deiced before departure. During flap retraction after takeoff the slats failed to come up so we stayed in the traffic pattern to circle and land. The Flight Engineer asked me if I wanted him to call maintenance and I said, "Not right now. Let's finish the after takeoff checklist, then run the abnormal checklist and then go right into the before landing checklist."

One of the first things learned in flight school is that you fly the airplane first then talk if you have time. When you are flying in heavy weather with a mechanical problem and configuring for landing, it's not a good time to distract yourself with a superfluous radio call. In addition, our General Operations Manual or GOM specifically prohibited any unnecessary radio calls other than to ATC when operating below 10,000 feet. Once the FAA approves an airline's operating criteria it becomes law. Making a radio call while we were below 10,000 feet could get me violated by the Feds for operating outside the confines of the GOM and possibly for exercising bad judgement.

After the airplane was repaired we completed both legs of the trip and arrived at our layover hotel several hours late. Being off duty long enough to meet the legally required amount of rest time meant that we wouldn't be able to show for the outbound leg of the flight in time enough to get out of Boston before the curfew or even make it to Cincinnati in time for the package sort.

We called crew scheduling to see if they wanted us to bring the trip back in that late or if there was a new plan. We were told that we were off duty and were being replaced on the inbound leg. A replacement crew was being flown in to take the flight. I was to have an airline ticket back to Cincinnati and the other two crew members would ride in on the jump seats of the DHL aircraft. I finally got into bed a little after 2:00 PM.

Crew scheduling called and woke me up at 3:45 just a couple of hours after our rest period had started. They wanted us to head to the airport for a 9:30 PM show time to take the inbound flight that evening. I initially thought that the original crew schedulers must have gone home and that a new shift of schedulers hadn't been briefed about us being off duty. The crew scheduler on the phone explained that due to the weather, the flight that was to bring our replacement crew was unable to make it to Bradley and that the 9:30 PM show time would meet minimum rest requirements. I expressed my concern about the pending noise curfew violation and said I would get back to them after I meet with the other crew members to see if we were all rested enough to take the trip inbound now that our rest had been interrupted by the call.

It didn't make me feel any better to know that I was right about the weather causing problems with the inbound leg of the trip. I knew that these kind of problems were like a snowball rolling down a hill. They just keep getting bigger and causing more damage.

After talking with the other crew members I called scheduling back and told them we all felt rested enough to be able to bring the flight in but we were all still concerned about the noise curfew at Boston. I was told that they were sending another aircraft to Boston to cover that part of the trip and we would be operating to Cincinnati through Detroit so the curfew wouldn't be a problem.

Upon our arrival at the airport that evening we noticed that the paper work for the trip indicated the normal routing through Boston. I naturally assumed that the dispatcher on duty was unaware of the change in flight plans and had sent the wrong routing. When I called dispatch to have them send a new flight plan I was told that those were correct. We really were expected to operate through Boston.

One could accept that weather had kept us from being replaced but this kind of mistake began to look like we had been presented with a deliberate falsehood in order to get us to show up for the trip. During my conversation with dispatch they claimed to be unaware that we had an airplane that didn't meet the noise requirements for the trip. I told dispatch that we would need some type of assurance that we wouldn't be prosecuted for the noise curfew violation during the Boston leg of the trip as mentioned in the memo put out by Gene and they had me talk to Pumpkin Head. He claimed that he was never aware of any plan for us to return through Detroit but he did fax us a letter pledging legal representation and payment of any fines by the company in the event of our being prosecuted by the State of Massachusetts.

System Operations Control, Crew Scheduling and Dispatch literally sat facing each other in the same room and still couldn't communicate or coordinate with each other. Their actions consistently displayed what could only by considered either incompetence or subterfuge. Either way, we had been finessed into taking the trip.

It had been snowing all day and we needed deiced before flying to Boston so after we blocked out we taxied to the deice pad. The deice truck started spraying us at about 12:30 AM Eastern time and after a few minutes, with only a part of one wing done, it promptly ran out of deice fluid. The deice truck operator told us he would go get more fluid and come back. Two hours later we were told it would be just another twenty minutes or so. A half hour after that we were told that they didn't know how long it would be before they could come back to deice us.

We were unable to reach dispatch by radio from where we were parked so we had the mechanic go back to his office and call them on the land line to fill them in on the latest excitement. The deice procedure that had taken over three hours so far had caused us to miss the sort so the company had us taxi back to the ramp, released us from duty and sent us to the hotel.

We got to the hotel at about 6:00 AM and I laid down to get some sleep. Todd from crew scheduling called me at 6:35 AM and said they wanted us to go to the airport to ferry the aircraft to Cincinnati at 9AM. This time the new shift at crew scheduling actually was totally unaware of what had been going on. When I explained that we had just gotten back to the hotel Todd said he had no idea we had been on duty all night. He thought we had been at the hotel sleeping so he told me to get some sleep and said they would call later. In an attempt to avoid any additional untimely interruptions I unplugged my phone in hopes of getting some actual sleep.

At 2:00 PM hotel security knocked on my door waking me up to let me know that DHL had been trying to reach me by phone and wanted me to call crew scheduling. I called them and found out they wanted us to head to the airport as soon as possible to fly directly to Cincinnati. The urgency in the scheduler's voice indicated that this was one of those type of situations where an aircraft had gotten out of place because of mechanical or weather problems and the company was anxious about getting it back to Cincinnati as soon as possible to be available for an outbound trip.

I got ahold of the other guys to tell them what the company wanted and we all got dressed and down to the lobby as soon as we could. We were all of the mind that it would be nice to get home early with a midday departure straight to Cincinnati after having our rest interrupted so frequently over the last two days. Our efforts to hurry got us to the airport at 3:00 PM all set to head home. Then we looked at the paper work.

The flight plan sent by dispatch showed us going to Boston with the second leg scheduled to leave Boston for Cincinnati at 10:42 PM. Not only were we not going direct to Cincinnati but now there would be a six hour wait for departure time once we landed in Boston. Yet again they had interrupted our sleep and rushed us to the airport to conduct a flight that had no resemblance to what we were told we would be doing. Knowing that it was probably an exercise in futility, I called to see if there was some mistake and was not surprised to learn that we were indeed going through Boston.

During our down time at Boston the company called to let us know that we needed to meet with the Flight Manager once we landed in Cincinnati. I had been at DHL for seven or so years at this point and had learned a couple of things. One of which was that flight Managers don't invite you to their offices to offer you tea and crumpets. Before we left Boston I called the union to make sure we would have representation at the meeting. After landing in Cincinnati we went to the meeting and were asked to lay out what we had experienced over the course of the last three days. The meeting seemed innocuous enough, but of course things are never what they seem.

I was scheduled to be off for the next week so I went home and waited for the ax to fall. It fell a couple days later in the form of a call from Grim requesting that I drive to Cincinnati to meet with him the following day to discuss the events of the problematic three day ordeal so that a course of action could be decided upon.

It was known by the pilot group that Grim had what he called a "coaching file." He would compile information on various "undesirables" in J. Edgar Hoover fashion so that he would have ammunition with which to bludgeon them when a disciplinary situation arose. It was a practice which along with his Romanesque zeal for seeing pilots fed to the lions would ultimately get him ousted from the Chief Pilot position by management but unfortunately not before he was able to exact an uncomfortable measure of his tyrannical judgment.

I got to Grim's office and he had me sit down and wait for him while he completed some imaginary task. It was a tired old ploy that Grim probably saw in some movie and was designed to elevate the manager's status in the eyes of his hapless victim. He returned to his office for our discussion but was unsatisfied with my recounting of the crew's attempt to comply with the memo about the noise curfew in Boston saying, "Well, it's funny what we remember, isn't it?" His voice had that sing song lilt that was reminiscent of the old school yard taunt of "nanny, nanny, boo boo." He continued, "You couldn't remember the memo we put out advising you to give maintenance a call in the event of a turn back to the airport, could you?"

It became apparent that his questions were rhetorical and I wasn't there for a discussion, I was there to be sentenced. A letter listing the disciplinary actions the company was going to take had already been produced. Grim pulled a copy of the letter from a file in his desk and handed it to me. It could have just as easily been mailed saving me the trip to Grim's office which served no purpose other than to provide him with some perverse type of entertainment like a little boy pulling the wings off of a fly.

In the letter I was accused of failing to notify maintenance of a return to the airport during our mechanical problem and of being insubordinate for balking at the company's request that I break the noise curfew at Boston. The letter further laid out the penalties for my perceived crimes which included a 30 day suspension without pay, ten hours of additional IOE to be completed before returning to fly the line and I would need to complete an eight hour course on CRM (Cockpit Resource Management). It was hoped, the letter said, that I would use the time off to reflect upon the reasons for this discipline.

I reflected all right, straight to the office of a labor attorney where we had a very meaningful time of reflection. I understood that since we had union representation, Federal law dictated that the remedy for the company's unjust disciplinary actions would come through the grievance process. The reason I had the visit with the labor attorney was because I felt that I had been singled out for harassment. While he said that I had a great case that we were more than likely to win, he encouraged me to calculate what I felt I could earn by completing my career and weigh that against what we felt we could get from the suit.

With the knowledge that I could take effective legal action if needed, I was able to promise myself that I would never again put up with that type of treatment. They had created a monster.

In society if someone feels that they have been wronged they can file a law suit in an attempt to have that wrong corrected. When there is a contractual agreement between management and labor with a union involved, the solution for contractual infractions or disputed disciplinary actions is for the person who felt they had been wronged to file a grievance. The grievance process can take a bit of time.

While I felt my grievance case was solid enough that I would ultimately be successful in getting my pay back and having the disciplinary letter removed from my records, the process would take long enough that I would have already completed the other penalties. I met with the Director of Operations before the grievance hearings got started and asked if he could hold off on the financial penalty until after the grievance was decided. My reasoning was that it could prevent the dual actions of taking my money and then having to pay it back since there was the possibility I would prevail. He assured me that they wouldn't take my pay until he had met with me and that we could make a payment plan that wouldn't cause me any serious complications.

Money was a little tight since I had recently gone through a divorce and was a single parent with custody of my two young daughters. The next week was my time off so I was at home when payday came around but there was no pay in my payday. I called the company to see if it was as a result of the disciplinary action even though the Director of Operations had assured me they would wait. Neither the Director of Operations nor the System Chief Pilot were available so I had to leave a message with the office secretary.

My eleven year old daughter and I went to the store and when we got home that evening the message light on the phone was blinking. Before I had a chance to stop her, she ran up and pushed the message button and I heard Grim's voice say, "Hi Kim, this is Grim, the reason you didn't get paid is because we fined you this week instead of waiting."

My daughter looked up at me almost in tears and asked, "Daddy, what happened? Aren't they going to pay you any more?"

No one likes to see their children worry. It took a bit of explaining but I was finally able to convince her it was just a mistake that would be corrected. It is shameful that Grim couldn't muster even the tiniest bit of social grace to have left a simple message asking me to return his call. Instead he left sensitive personal information on a medium that could be heard by anyone.

When I called Grim back to ask why the fine had been levied now instead of later as I was told it would be, he uncaringly said, "Yeah I decided to go ahead and do it now."

If you do things by the book you will usually be fine. I had done things by the book. I had followed the GOM, the FAR's and the company memos. All of that was borne out as I suspected it would be during the grievance process. It took a total of two years and several grievance hearings but I got my money back and the disciplinary letter was removed from my file. The fact that I had suffered the humiliation of doing extra IOE and taking the CRM class could not be undone but during the course of the two years it took to correct everything else we were able to bring several things to light.

We showed that several Flight Managers failed to communicate with other departments in planning and assigning trips and failed to accomplish even the simplest of tasks that could have prevented much of the late arrivals and confusion. Crew Scheduling was unable to properly assign crews to trips planned by Dispatch. Even after making assignments they were unable to track what assignments had been given and consequently interrupted required rest periods. Dispatch was either totally incompetent in planning trips required by the company or lied about the destinations and departure times to cause the flight crew to commit to completing a lesser trip in order to have them in position to be given the trip originally desired by the company. It was also learned that the memo that caused the initial concern about personal prosecution was in error. The State of Massachusetts confirmed that no individual would have been prosecuted. No one knows for sure why the false information had been included in the memo. It was generally assumed that Gene felt he couldn't command the desired level of cooperation and compliance without resorting to the cheap thuggery of exaggeration.

A flight crew was needlessly harassed, abused and disciplined even though they did their job according to proper procedures and made the extra effort to meet the excessive and often unreasonable demands of the company. Throughout this ordeal, flights were delayed, poorly equipped and improperly planned yet not a single one of the individuals actually responsible for this fiasco was ever held accountable for their misdeeds. The result of all this incompetence and stupidity was that the company and the union had to spend two years and tens of thousands of dollars defending their positions.

Chapter Seven

Straight From Central Casting

Shakespeare would have us believe that, "All the world's a stage and all the men and women merely players." During my time at DHL I saw all kinds of characters come and go. Some were funny and some were tragic but none of them could be ignored.

Wardrobe is an important part of any production. No Oscars for wardrobe would have been given to our uniform designers. We were originally dressed in what would more likely be considered a costume rather than a uniform. They were an impossible to keep clean, light brown color with dark brown stripes on the sleeves and the hat was light brown with a dark brown bill. The overall effect was that we looked like a doorman or a bell hop instead of a pilot. There were times while standing outside the hotel waiting for our ride to the airport, people would approach us expecting us to carry their bags into the lobby for them. More than a couple of our pilots did so and supplemented their income with the tips they received. Wisdom eventually prevailed and we switched to an industry standard dark blue uniform that we could wear in public without being embarrassed.

While still a First Officer on the Boeing 727 I liked bidding the Caribbean charters that we flew out of JFK. The routing usually took us down the East coast of the U.S. before turning Eastward to our destination. One week I was paired with a Captain named Mike who was in the Air Force Reserve as a navigator. Suffice it to say, he knew his way around a chart.

Mike had a set of colored pencils that he would use to make various notes and markings on his charts about fixes and distances from navigation aids as we flew along. On the return leg he offered to let me borrow his colored pencils so I could make similar notations on my charts. I said, "No thanks, I'm fine," but noticed that he was visibly upset at my rejection of his offer so I continued, "we can see the coast right there. It's not like we're going to get lost."

He looked at me with sort of a pout and said, "You know, you're lazy," and I had to stifle a laugh.

Mike had one of those last names that you had to practice in order to say it properly. It was made up of a whole bunch of consonants with a couple of Y's thrown in. Some may consider Y's to be a vowel but we're using the "Wheel of Fortune" rules here. The overhead lights in the 727 cockpit had little dome shaped covers over the bulbs and guys would take them off and write messages in them so when you got in the cockpit and turned on the light you would see the message. I got in the airplane and turned on the overhead lights once to see the message, "Mike, buy a vowel."

Messages in the overhead lights weren't the only thing left in the airplane for the next guy to enjoy. There were plenty of places like the access door to the fuel dump panel and other little access panels that could be popped out with just your finger to find a folded up piece of paper which would usually turn out to be a picture pulled out of...well, let's call it a gentleman's magazine.

I eventually married the girl friend that had so enjoyed watching my sim session and she was the manager of a travel agency. She mentioned to me one night that she had hired a new agent named Angel from Las Vegas. It was just during one of our normal conversations and I didn't think much of it until I was at work the following week and one of the guys checked the cubby holes to see what pictures were new and exciting.

He was looking at the picture of a blond posing on her kitchen counter in the all together and read the caption which said, "Angel is a travel agent in Las Vegas." I took the picture from him to check it out and thought to myself, "No, it couldn't be."

When we got to the hotel that morning I called my wife. "Hey honey, did you say that girl you hired was from Las Vegas?"

"Yes."

"Did you say her name is Angel?"

"Yes."

"She doesn't happen to have blond hair, does she?"

"Well, yeah. Why do you ask?"

"I think I just saw her picture in a magazine," I said not wanting to just blurt out that she was posing nude.

"What do you mean?" she asked.

I explained that the picture was from the section of a nudie magazine that featured personal pictures sent in by readers and then of course had to explain how I happened to have come into possession of such an item.

My wife mentioned this to the two brothers that owned the travel agency she managed and they immediately went out and bought the magazine. Sure enough, it was Angel. The two walked through the office for the next couple weeks singing, "Angel Is The Centerfold" over my wife's protestations. She also made sure I knew that she didn't want any of my pilot buddies showing up at the travel agency pretending to need travel advice.

In the eighties, airlines tried lowering pay scales through a combination of bankruptcies and contract negotiations. The result was that new hires at some airlines were given a new, lower rate of pay called "B" scale pay. One night I opened one of the panels to find a stick figure drawn showing breasts made of two circles with dots in the middle. The caption at the bottom said, "B scale porn."

One of the attractions to an airline career was the ability to live anywhere you wanted and still be able to get to work by jump seating. About seventy-five percent of our pilot group were commuters. Most airlines had reciprocal jump seat agreements and allowed pilots from other carriers to catch a ride on their jump seats.

I didn't use jump seats a lot but always carried my ID when traveling in case I would need to catch a ride somewhere. Shortly before my wife and I got married we took a trip to Jamaica. While travel agents don't get free tickets much any more, she used to get some tremendous deals. I had just finished my Captain upgrade and this was the first trip the two of us had taken together.

We were on an American Airlines A-300 out of Miami to Montego Bay. After we got to our seats I told my girlfriend Kathy I wanted to go say hi to the crew and check out the cockpit. I stuck my head in the cockpit, showed my ID and told them I flew an old 727 and wanted to see what a nice new airplane looked like. The Captain was friendly and said, "Well why don't you ride up here with us for the takeoff and then go back to your seat for the rest of the flight?" I went back to the seat to tell Kathy that I was going to ride in the cockpit for takeoff and would come back and join her after that.

I was a smoker at the time and this was back when you could still smoke on international flights. After we were airborne the Captain said, "Let's have a cup of coffee and a smoke." We drank coffee, smoked and talked airplanes until it was time to start our descent into Jamaica. As we started down, the flight attendant came into the cockpit and said, "Uh…your girlfriend wanted to know if you were going to come back to your seat."

When I got back to my seat I expected to suffer the wrath of a woman scorned but Kathy offered a good natured smile and said, "Well at least I know where I stand with airplanes."

The return trip was also on an American A-300 but I wouldn't risk any further damage to my new relationship with Kathy by sitting up front this time. I did stop by the cockpit just to be polite and say hello. Our ID's had the name of our airline and the words "Flight Crew" in bold print along with our picture. I offered it to the Captain and said, "Hi, I'm a 727 Captain with DHL. I wanted to say hi before I headed back to my seat."

He looked at my ID, made a little snorting sound and handed it back to me saying, "What are you, a flight attendant?"

I managed to not react too negatively to the intentional slam and answered, "You know we're a freight carrier and don't have flight attendants, don't you?"

Of course he had known but he just said, "I suggest you go back to your seat and enjoy the flight."

As soon as I got to my seat I made note of his name so I could pass it and a recounting of his antics along to the jump seat committee at ALPA. It wouldn't affect him at American Airlines since they had a different union but if he ever tried to get a jump seat on an ALPA carrier his hospitality would be properly repaid.

Every airline had their share of "Sky Gods" like the one I met on that flight. They all displayed an attitude that let you know they were God's gift to Aviation. Kathy had an encounter with one as she was getting ready to board an American Airlines flight to San Diego one afternoon. She was waiting to hear about an upgrade on her ticket when a man in a pilot uniform came up to the gate agent and said he was dead heading on the flight. As he sat down near Kathy she struck up a conversation. "My husband is an A-300 Captain for DHL," she said. "Are you with American?"

"Yes," he answered, "I'm an A-300 Captain as well." Then he asked, "Did your husband ever think about coming to American and flying with the "Big Boys"?"

While she didn't appreciate the implication that her husband flew for a lesser carrier she simply said, "No, he has it too good where he is."

He told her what he made at American offering the unspoken suggestion that it was certainly more than what a freight pilot would make.

If he wanted to dig a hole, she was going to give him the shovel. "My husband makes about forty-thousand more than that," she said, "he wouldn't want to take a pay cut."

"Well, we have a great schedule. I have three or four days off after a short work week," he continued.

"My husband works a week on and a week off. He would't want to give that up."

"Well, we get three weeks of vacation a year," he said still thinking he could convince her he really had it made.

"My husband gets four weeks and if he bids his schedule right he can turn that into twelve weeks off," she said almost starting to feel bad for the guy.

"Our retirement plan is one of the best," he contributed weakly.

"The DHL 401k plan contributes 15%. I really don't think my husband would want to go to an "A" plan."

"Yeah it sounds like he has a pretty good deal there," he said not offering any further evidence that the "Big Boys" had it so much better.

Jump seating on DHL to and from work had it's own protocol. There was nothing written or official but everyone understood what was expected. If you were a DHL pilot riding to work on a DHL flight, you brought tribute for the crew operating the flight. That tribute would be in the form of food. Everybody loved having something good to eat on the flight.

The absolute king of tribute was Rick. He was practically a professional eater. We called him Rick Landfill which was a play on his real name because he could eat so much. If you were on a flight with

Rick you were going to enjoy a full buffet including bread, toppings, cold cuts and all the trimmings. The man could really put out a spread.

Tribute was rarely anything other than food except in the case of one of the most legendary Captains to fly for DHL, The Skipper. The Skipper would accept your tribute but if you were going to ride on his airplane there were a few other things you had to accomplish. He would have you "bless" the flight. This would happen just after he had given the crew a flight briefing and to do it you would smack your fist to your chest gladiator fashion and say, "So it is written, so let it be done."

Leaving the Skipper's airplane you would need to buckle your seat belt, pull it tight on the top of the seat and wrap the excess portion of belt neatly around the buckle. Even though this was all in fun, it was sometimes difficult to know just how serious the Skipper was. After some complaints he was asked to tone it down. If you were a part of Skipper's crew he liked you to do things in a very specific way. He was happy to show you how he wanted it done and if you asked, he would explain why it should be done that way. Surprisingly, he seemed to always have a good reason.

One night in the crew lounge at our hub, the Skipper was entertaining a circle of listeners telling the story of an airplane he was familiar with that was previously owned by a famous actor who had died some time ago. The name of the famous person and the fact that he had owned this airplane was overheard by one of our young female pilots but she had missed the part about him being dead. She went up to the Skipper and asked if that person still flew his airplane. The Skipper answered in his ex-Marine, barking voice, "No. He lost his medical."

A professional pilot spends a lot of time in training and good instructors can mean the difference between failure and success. We were lucky to have Danny in our training department. Danny was a curator of information on aircraft, weather, aviation accidents and just about anything else that may need to be looked at or studied. Sitting in one of his classes experiencing his soft spoken delivery and his dark framed glasses you would be tempted to think of him as a frail, book worm professor type. You would be wrong. Before coming to DHL as a ground school instructor Danny flew in the Reno Air Races. During one race he encountered some wake turbulence at 200 knots and crashed. The airplane was torn apart and totaled but Danny walked away with only a minor scratch from having tripped over the throttle cable that was still attached to the engine which was lying on the ground outside of the cowling. As Danny stood there looking at the wreckage, the rescue squad drove up and noticing the empty cockpit, asked Danny, "Have you seen the pilot?"

That day didn't end like he may have wanted but a few years later he won the National Championship Air Races in Reno.

Keith had been in the training department since before I joined DHL. We all knew him as the Absent Minded Professor. He was a great instructor and knew his material very well but could still show up at work wearing two different colored socks.

After 9-11 the government instituted the FFDO program. Flight crew members who volunteered would be trained at a federal facility to become Federal Flight Deck Officers and would be armed while on duty in the cockpit. Keith became an FFDO. There were strict guidelines for those in the program concerning where and how their weapons could be carried. One restriction was that they couldn't be taken on international flights.

The Absent Minded Professor found himself on one of our Mexico trips and only after somehow making it through customs did he realize he was carrying his weapon. It was rumored that he disassembled the weapon and deposited the parts in various trash cans to avoid complications with security and customs when returning to the aircraft for the trip back to the states. He had to buy a new gun when he got back.

Guns were often a topic of discussion among the pilot group since several of the group were gun owners. Pilots are typically deliberate in how they approach any task which usually translates into a measure of safety. On one occasion however, several pilots were on reserve status at their crash pad looking at and discussing hand guns. A crash pad is an apartment or home shared by several pilots who typically commute but need an occasional place to stay near their base of operations. One of the pilots on reserve was demonstrating his hand gun and pulled the trigger accidentally shooting one of the other pilots in the stomach. The injured pilot ultimately recovered and the trigger man was not disciplined by the company.

It was a short time after the shooting incident that there was a dispute in the cockpit between two other crew members. It was the last leg of the trip which was a very short flight from Seattle to

Portland. During descent, the First Office put his hand on the gear lever in preparation to lower the gear as soon as the proper speed was reached. The Captain who was flying that leg of the trip mistakenly thought the FO was going to lower the gear before it was called for and slapped the FO's hand away from the lever. That Captain was fired after the FO complained about being struck. It therefore became conventional wisdom at DHL that when dealing with other crew members, you could shoot them, you just couldn't slap them.

Not all legends were of the good kind. There always seems to be one that slips through the cracks and gets hired contrary to all the signs indicating they shouldn't have been. Spanky should never have been hired. There were some glaring issues that didn't surface in the interview but later showed up in the form of a couple of convictions for exposing himself, which is why the pilot group ultimately dubbed him Spanky. He evidently wasn't a very skillful flasher since he had gotten caught twice, once in Florida and once in Texas.

In what I can only guess must have been an attempt to perfect the flawed technique that had resulted in two previous convictions, he went for the hat trick. The poor, unlucky stiff (yeah, I know) decided to rub one out in front of the wrong person. The target of his display was a girl that happened to be married to a DHL aircraft mechanic. Her husband accompanied her to the police station to look at mug shots and when the wife picked Spanky out of the line up, the husband recognized him as one of the DHL pilots and Spanky was busted again. Surprisingly, that didn't get him fired.

Being around Spanky was never comfortable. If you had dinner with him, the noises he would make while eating would cause people to turn and look at you. On one occasion I thought I might get called into the Chief Pilot's office after he made crude comments to women as we stood outside of JFK in uniform waiting for the hotel van to pick us up.

He flew with me as a First Officer a few times and as he talked to ATC on the radio using a deliberate, dramatically low voice I experienced a feeling of eerie familiarity. It finally dawned on me that he sounded like I did as a young boy sitting in a cardboard box I had drawn fake instruments on so I could pretend to fly. Here he was at thirty some thousand feet flying a wide body jet but in his mind just pretending to be an airline pilot. After all of that and having to council him about the improper takeoff method he employed, I avoided flying with him by bidding the schedules I knew he wouldn't be flying.

The proper procedure during takeoff was to pull the yoke back at a slow and steady rate and the aircraft would fly off of the ground but Spanky would yank violently on the yoke and jerk the aircraft off. (Yeah, I did it again.)

Spanky did that once while flying with another Captain and that Captain refused to fly with Spanky any further after they landed. The company had to send a relief crew out to LAX to pick up the airplane and finish the trip. Spanky was sent to the sim for remedial training during which he was able to demonstrate that he did know how to do it properly so he was fired for deliberately doing it wrong in the airplane.

Executives of all sizes and shapes came and went as DHL tried to find the right person or combination of them to manage the airline. One came in with a team of people made up mostly of ex-United managers of various types. They had a "meet the team" open house and handed out some cup cakes. A few weeks later the guy died of a heart attack and DHL had to go get another leader.

One great leader came in and immediately wrote a company mission statement that we all had to learn. To me a mission statement is like an appendix. It doesn't really do anything but if it gets messed up it can cause problems. I don't really remember what our mission statement said but it should have been, "We fly packages." Boom. It's to the point and keeps you focused.

Some people come from a business that just doesn't translate to the airline business. One of our imported executives came from a company that made window blinds. Pilots are required to carry a set of charts in their flight bags to use for navigating and making approaches for landings. In a demonstration of his lack of aviation savvy the window blind guy suggested saving money by only paying for one set of charts to be kept in the pilot lounge for the pilots to refer to as opposed to each of them carrying a set.

An aggressive executive can sometimes go a bit too far as they make changes to affect the bottom line and impress their superiors. This happened at DHL as well.

Employees of DHL were given between one and four weeks of vacation per year depending on their time with the company and everyone also had five floating holidays that could be used any time. The pilots had schedules that were made up of seven days on and seven days off of flying duty or reserve duty but the two weren't mixed together. That type of schedule was sacred to the flight crews as it facilitated the bidding of vacations, time off and commuting to and from work.

One executive showed up and thought he would make his mark by killing our sacred cow. He took away the pilot's floating holidays, mixed reserve days in with flying lines and began breaking up the seven on, seven off schedules. He also decided that when a regular employee took a week of vacation, they were really only taking five days off so the four weeks of vacation available to a senior employee was really just twenty days. This convoluted way of thinking allowed him to steel over a quarter of the pilot group's vacation time by claiming that when a pilot took a week off he was using seven of his vacation days instead of just five.

Almost every airline gets to a point where there is union talk. It is usually initiated as the result of conditions created by management that cause the pilot group to feel that they are losing pay, benefits or favorable working conditions. The pilot group at DHL had reached that point.

There had been union talk before but it wasn't strong enough to cause ALPA (The Air Line Pilots Association) to want to sponsor an attempt to organize at DHL. ALPA felt that while we may be able to get enough cards signed to legally force a vote, interest wouldn't be strong enough that an actual union vote would be successful. The talk was much stronger this time. Management had gone too far with what they had taken away and there would be a price to pay.

The company took the typical steps to combat union organization such as sending anti union videos to everyone and holding a few ineffective meetings. They finally decided to feign an attempt to give the pilot group a voice by offering pseudo representation with what they called the "Flight Crew Supplement Committee."

The Flight Crew Supplement was an addendum to the Employee Handbook that addressed the differences in working conditions and situations unique to flight crews. This committee was to be elected by the pilot group and would meet regularly with management so the two sides could come to some mutually agreed upon way to boost productivity and meet the pilots' needs as well. I was one of the five elected to the Flight Crew Supplement Committee.

The company had hired a new executive and the committee was to meet and coordinate with him. I don't remember his title but he could just as easily have been called the Vice President In Charge Of Keeping The Pilot Group Distracted. He told the committee that the pilot group had to be more productive. We stressed to him that the seven on, seven off schedule was sacred.

During the months that the committee was active, we met in hotel rooms and in the house of one of the members and spent hours and hours developing schedules that kept the week on, week off structure but also increased the number of hours flown in each schedule. Those proposed schedules had been presented to the company but a few days later we met with the VP and were told that the company had been working for several weeks on developing some schedules of their own that were going to be adopted instead of the ones we had presented. The company's schedules showed about the same productivity as ours but only a couple of them were seven on, seven off.

I looked at the VP and said, "You led us to believe our input would be considered but have been developing your own schedules the whole time with no intention of using our input. This committee is a complete sham." I got up and walked out.

All of us on the committee were angry at having been used as a diversion while the company just implemented what they had wanted all along. We decided to form our own union that we called The DHL Pilots Association and went about collecting enough signatures to cause a vote for union representation. As we passed out the cards for signatures we told people that they could write in ALPA as the union they wanted to represent them explaining that a start up union would be extremely expensive and probably not very effective. The pilot group responded positively and so started our affiliation with The Air Line Pilots Association.

Shortly after all of this the VP that had been meeting with us "left to take advantage of other opportunities" as they say when middle management gets fired. We never knew but it was generally assumed that his job was to keep a union from forming and he had failed so he was no longer needed at DHL.

The most legendary of all characters at DHL was Larry Hillblom, the H in DHL. He started the company with Adrian Dalsey and Robert Lynn, the D and L. Books have been written about Larry Hillblom and the major television networks have produced magazine shows exposing his antics and those of the company after his death. It is all very fascinating and much of what went on affected everyone at DHL as well as his heirs.

Hillblom was an attorney by trade before starting DHL. He liked the South Pacific and moved to Saipan, one of the main islands in the Marianas where he was a very popular figure. He eventually became a judge there as well.

Being an airplane enthusiast, he got his pilot license and bought a sea plane that he liked to fly. By all accounts he wasn't a very good pilot and crashed his sea plane twice. He survived the first mishap, but died as a result of the second one on May 21, 1995. His body was never recovered causing a shortage of DNA information that would eventually be wanted for several law suits. In the Marianas, law suits were filed against Hillblom's estate by parents of children reportedly fathered by Larry. In the rest of the world the ownership status of the privately held DHL empire had to be determined. It really is amazing how one person's death can affect so many people so dramatically all across the globe.

One of the potential heirs to the Hillblom estate was a boy who had been named Junior Larry Hillbroom (yes it is spelled correctly) by his mother, Kaelani Kinney who had had an affair with Hillblom. Kinney brought suit against Hillblom's estate and fortunately had a tenacious attorney who refused to give up on the case which ultimately resulted in an award of about fifty-million dollars. The suit faced a tremendous amount of opposition not only because Hillblom's body was never recovered but also because all other forms of DNA went missing for a time.

In an attempt to prevent large portions of his estate from being divvied up among those claiming to be heirs, a few upper level executives close to Hillblom at the time of his death attempted to keep DNA information from entering the legal proceedings through various deceptive methods. They poured acid down the drains at Hillblom's home and buried his clothing and personal effects so no DNA could be found. Even a mole of Larry's that had been removed a few years earlier mysteriously disappeared from a California hospital.

The efforts at evidence tampering ultimately failed. A back hoe operator was hired to dig up Hillblom's yard in an attempt to find the buried articles. He knew right where to dig since he was the only back hoe operator on the island and had originally been hired to bury the items.

The news of these goings on gave us a better understanding of what had conditioned and shaped the corporate culture we constantly faced. However, it didn't make us feel any better to know that we worked for the kind of people who were capable of such a frightening level of subterfuge.

It has always been said that you should be careful what you wish for. The pilot group had seen it happen before when a new manager proved to be worse than the despot they replaced. We would see it happen again with a change of ownership since after Larry Hillblom's death the once privately held company ended up in the hands of Deutsche Post and began a new era of highly sophisticated, German engineered stupidity.

The fact that the new owner of DHL was a German company and that U.S. law doesn't allow a foreign entity to own more than 49 percent of an American certified air carrier created a problem.

The solution was to have the airline portion of DHL spun off as a separate company operating as an airline flying under contract to DHL. We therefore became DHL Airways which included the pilots, mechanics, aircraft, crew scheduling department and dispatch along with some administrative personnel.

It was a perfectly simple and logical solution that met the requirement of the law and was all legally and properly done. Unfortunately UPS who had their own fleet of aircraft by this time and Fed Ex decided to file suit claiming that DHL still exercised operational control over the airline and were therefore operating illegally.

In an effort to combat the legal complications imposed by the Fed Ex and UPS law suit, DHL sold DHL Airways to a group of investors headed by John Dasburg. Dasburg's group had a law firm with a prestigious Washington D.C. address and Dasburg himself had been the former CEO of Northwest Airlines.

It was a move that was pretty much a case of DHL saying, "That'll shut 'em up," and it had the desired effect. The legal issues were dealt with and DHL Airways became Astar Air Cargo (pronounced with a long "A" sound).

The legal complications hadn't hampered DHLs growth. The first few years of the new century brought plans for a new hub and sort center to be built at the south end of the Cincinnati airport. There were wonderful rumors of bigger and better facilities such as a better cafeteria, a nicer pilot's lounge and so forth. As we watched it being built and looked forward to moving into it, there were other rumors circulating as well. We kept hearing talk of DHL buying Airborne Express.

The day finally came when we moved into the new facility and it was wonderful. Everything in the sort center was fully automated and it was reported that the total capacity of the sort was more than twice what it had been before. Giant screens showing weather and routing maps made the dispatch department look like something out of a James Bond movie. Pilots were treated to quiet bunk rooms for those that wanted to catch a nap and comfortable recliners in the pilot lounge for TV viewing or reading. Even catching the van that took us out to the aircraft was more comfortable with a covered waiting area that protected us from the elements.

I was thankful for the cover protecting me from the rain as I waited for a ride to the Airbus for my LA flight one night. Thunder storms were expected to the west of Cincinnati and I had concerns about our onboard weather radar. There had been complaints about it not showing weather accurately. It was later learned that the radar problems had been caused by the wrong type of paint having been used on the nose cone covering the radar antenna blocking its ability to receive a proper return signal. The radome problem would eventually be fixed but that didn't help me on this flight.

We took off for Los Angeles with a full load of cargo and about eighty-thousand pounds of fuel and started climbing to our planned altitude of over thirty-thousand feet. We were in the clouds but there was nothing showing on the radar for us to avoid. As we climbed through about fifteen thousand feet we got into a heavy rain that caused some extreme noise as it hit the aircraft. The rain got heavier and louder until it was the loudest noise I had ever heard. It sounded like the aircraft was being pelted with thousands of bricks and it dawned on me that we were being pounded by hail. It was not the little quarter inch type of hail you might see during a summer day's storm but thousands of softball size stones judging by the sound of it and the dents we later saw on the nose and leading edges of the wings. Of course being in the clouds at night going three hundred miles per hour, it wasn't anything you could see.

The noise was so loud it hurt your ears and you couldn't hear someone even if they yelled which is what I later learned my First Officer was doing. As I was just wrapping my brain around the fact that we were in the middle of the world's worst hail storm I felt a tap on my arm. I looked to the right and saw my FO crouched down and bent over in his seat with his head below the dash board pointing up at his windshield.

His windshield was shattered so badly that he thought it would break in on him at any moment. The Flight Engineer must have been thinking the same thing since he sat directly behind the FO and was also crouched down below windshield level. Then suddenly it was over. The cockpit was silent but our ears were ringing from the recent aural assault.

Now that we could talk and were out of the hail storm we had to assess the damage and make a plan. The FO's windshield was shattered and appeared to have three or four main points of impact. Even though it was over two and a half inches thick I could see why he was hesitant to keep his head up. I don't know how my side of the windshield had escaped unscathed.

We declared an emergency and told ATC we needed to return to Cincinnati and had them vector us to an area where we could dump enough fuel to get us down to our maximum landing weight. After completing all of the emergency checklists and once we had the fuel dump in progress I had the Engineer call the company to tell them what had happened and that we were returning. (In this situation we were above ten thousand feet, had already completed our required checklists and were actually on a flight that was returning to the airport as opposed to having remained in the traffic pattern like the time when I was persecuted for not calling the company.)

After a couple minutes on the radio with the company, the Flight Engineer said, "Hey Captain, they want us to go on to LA. They said it's in the book that we can still fly with a crack in the outer pane of the windshield. I don't think they understand."

I said to the First Officer, "You have the airplane." When he took the controls I got on the radio with maintenance and said, "We have a shattered windshield. We have declared an emergency. We are dumping fuel and are returning to Cincinnati. Do you have any questions?"

All they said after a couple seconds was, "OK, we'll see you in a few minutes."

We had depressurized and slowed down to under 250 knots and were able to get back to the airport without the windshield caving in on us. It was daylight by that time and the Flight Manager on duty along with several mechanics met us as we blocked in.

"Wow, you did the right thing coming back. You couldn't keep flying with that," the Flight Manager said as he took several pictures. I went inside to fill out the report that was required after having declared an emergency and gave a verbal report to the Manager before going home to get some sleep.

The way to the Chief Pilot and Flight Manager's offices was through the nice new pilot lounge and a fellow pilot had been relaxing in one of the recliners there while finishing his reserve shift. He later told me that shortly after I left, a fourth floor puke of some type had come storming through the pilot's lounge to the Chief Pilot's office in an uproar saying, "That Captain deliberately flew directly into a thunder storm. We should go after his license."

It was disturbing to think that we had people working in airline operations who knew so little about aviation that they could make such an irresponsible, uninformed statement. I was always thankful that I wasn't there to hear it or I might have done something stupid like slap him which as we know, would have gotten me fired.

Chapter Eight

Let Your Colors Fly

Deutsche Post decided they wanted to increase their market share in the overnight package business. At that time, DHL had about three and a half percent of the domestic business in the U.S. and Airborne Express had about twelve and a half percent. All of the rumors we had heard over the last few years now seemed to have some credibility. It was Deutsche Post's reasoning that if DHL bought Airborne, they would instantly have over fifteen percent of the market and wouldn't have to advertise and wait for the growth they wanted.

The reality was that Airborne Express was not that far from going Tango Uniform. At Astar Air Cargo we would have preferred to grow through advertising and even our CEO John Dasburg tried to reason with DHL suggesting that they simply wait, let Airborne go under and then pick up the pieces. Deutsche Post didn't wait. Instead, they had DHL buy Airborne Express with absolutely disastrous results that ultimately put tens of thousands of people out of work.

It is never easy merging two companies that were previously in competition with each other but the case of DHL buying Airborne was worse than normal. Along with the expected cultural differences, Airborne's equipment and infrastructure were totally incompatible not only with DHL but with the entire freight industry.

Airborne was a dinosaur on the brink of extinction and DHL was the meteor about ready to crash into its world.

Airborne operated several older DC-9 aircraft, a few DC-8 aircraft and some Boeing 767s. When Airborne Express started flight operations they only hauled their own packages so there was no need to be compatible with the rest of the cargo world. Consequently, they didn't go to the trouble and expense of converting their aircraft to a cargo configuration which would have included industry standard cargo doors and containers. Instead they reinvented the wheel by developing small, outhouse looking cargo containers that would fit through the passenger doors which they loaded using a conveyor belt contraption they also developed. It was a labor intensive, Fred Flintstone way of handling freight. In the speedy world of overnight packages their system was like running a horse drawn carriage in the Indy 500.

Now that Airborne was owned by a foreign entity, they too had to spin the airline portion off as a separate company. It became ABX Air and the rest of their company became DHL. ABX was based in Wilmington, Ohio operating out of the airport they owned which had previously been Clinton County Air Force Base. The Wilmington airport still looked like an Air Force Base out of the 1950s with an unorganized scattering of the original buildings and hangars now converted into offices or operations facilities. There was also a private control tower which was operated by Airborne.

Astar continued to operate out of DHL's new hub at Cincinnati and we thought we might be able to stay there since the airport at Wilmington didn't have any way to handle or load the industry standard cargo containers that we used. An actual merger of operations between ABX and Astar Air Cargo seemed impractical considering the differences in equipment and capabilities but we underestimated DHL's ability to cram square pegs into round holes. It wasn't long before we found ourselves getting used to another new facility only this one wasn't nearly as nice. By the time we moved to Wilmington we had only been able to enjoy our upscale facility in Cincinnati for a couple of years.

DHL had just spent over fifty-five million dollars on the fully automated hub it was abandoning in Cincinnati. They put an additional thirty-million into a makeshift, manually operated sort building at the Wilmington airport so that the industry standard freight containers could be handled. In addition it would cost DHL over one hundred million dollars a year just to operate the private airport in the middle of the corn fields of Ohio.

There was one thing that DHL was actually very good at and that was painting everything yellow. Every building at the Wilmington airport was painted in DHL colors including the control tower. The Airborne gray color scheme had been wiped out. It was a change of identity that didn't sit well with the Airborne faithful and they would make their displeasure known.

An estimated eighty percent of the population of Wilmington, Ohio now worked for DHL instead of Airborne. They held an emotional attachment to their previous company and expressed their displeasure with an irrational display of defiance. All of these employees still had the same job, doing the same thing at the same place, working with the same people for the same pay. The only thing that was different was the color of the paint and the name on the buildings. Any number of unemployed people throughout the country would have loved having a job but that didn't register with these folks.

There were several thousand DHL employees that weren't so lucky. The fact that Airborne Express had been close to going under could have been partially due to their antiquated equipment and methods but was almost certainly exacerbated by inept management. DHL in yet another display of the kind of wisdom that ruins companies decided to keep the Airborne management and fire the DHL faithful. Some of the thousands of employees that were let go had over twenty years with DHL. Those that lost their jobs included not only managers, loaders and office staff but also drivers who were the main contact that most of the customers had with DHL. The company errantly thought they would save money using the contract drivers that had been servicing Airborne deliveries. That decision proved disastrous when DHL customers failed to get the personal attention they had been used to and started shipping with other carriers.

DHL spent millions adding infrastructure like extra ramp space to accommodate the additional aircraft Astar Air Cargo would bring with them to Wilmington. Now, instead of parking on a ramp near the hub, we would park the aircraft in one of four ramps scattered all over the airport. They also converted a warehouse into our new offices, classrooms and pilot lounge. It wasn't what we were used to but it had a roof. It didn't have space for parking though so we had to use a remote parking lot and get bussed to the "new" ops building when we came to work. Nothing at Wilmington was modern or convenient.

The ramp personnel at Wilmington needed to be trained in handling and loading the containers that were used in our aircraft. DHL flew an Airbus and another airplane to Wilmington so they could be used for the training but very few of the ramp personnel bothered to show up for it.

As a result, for the first few weeks we operated out of Wilmington we suffered loading problems that resulted in departure delays of five or six hours on every flight every day. The delays often caused the flight crews to go over their duty time and need replacing. DHL started loosing a reported seventy-million dollars per week as well as a large portion of their market share totally negating the gains they had realized by the purchase of Airborne in the first place.

To fix the problem DHL had to offer some of their fired rampers from Cincinnati a premium in pay and provide transportation to and from Wilmington to entice them to come work with and train the Wilmington crews. It took a couple of months to get the situation under control.

Nothing worked out well for our Astar family at Wilmington. The die hard Airborne employees hated DHL and even though we were Astar and not DHL, we were perceived to have brought the yellow with us when we came so we were treated as if we were DHL. Some of our cars got keyed, a few windows were broken and some tires were slashed. Extra security was placed at the remote employee parking lot that both ABX and Astar Air Cargo employees used and the problem eventually cleared up.

Astar contracted with ABX for ground support which included loading, fueling, deicing and any other ramp services necessary and ABX employees operated the Air Traffic Control Tower at the airport as well. We were completely at their mercy. ABX flights were given preferential treatment for taxi and takeoff and if the sort was in a time crunch or running late we always got loaded last.

The overnight package business requires a tremendous amount of equipment to support ground and ramp operations. There are tugs to pull the trains that haul the containers to and from the aircraft. In addition, each parked aircraft requires a ground power unit or GPU, loaders for the main cargo door and belly cargo bins and stairs for the crew to reach the passenger entry door.

All of this equipment was loaded on a caravan of trucks and hauled up I-71 from Cincinnati when we moved to Wilmington and all of this equipment was fairly new and in good condition. All the Airborne equipment was old and in rough condition. Since DHL had contracted with ABX for the ground and ramp support it was like buying the chicken coop and then putting the fox in charge of security. Over time most of our good equipment was usurped by the ABX ramp workers and used for the ABX aircraft and we would pull into the blocks to find either old, broken down equipment or the wrong equipment waiting to service our aircraft.

I would pull into my assigned parking position on the ramp and there would be a small ground power unit designed for a DC-9 waiting for us instead of one that the A300 could use. We would have to keep the aircraft auxiliary power unit running burning extra fuel and making noise while the ramp workers went to find a GPU that could service our aircraft. It may seem like a small thing but when several aircraft are involved on a given night it could affect sort efficiency and ultimately cause delays in departures and deliveries.

Safety could be impacted by these equipment switches as well. Each aircraft used a different type of stairs for crew access. On the airbus we used a staircase that had three flights of eight or so steps. After the first eight steps there was a landing and the direction of the steps would reverse for the next eight steps to another landing and another direction reverse to a landing that was at the level of the entry door to the aircraft. The resulting vertical stair case was more stable than a straight set of stairs would be and didn't stick out onto the ramp creating an obstacle for ramp vehicles. We brought several nice new sets of stairs with us from Cincinnati. Airborne had a few similar types of stairs but they were old, rickety and home made looking and of course ended up being used on our airplanes.

ABX also had some long, straight, skinny, single flight stair sets that they used on some of their 767s. These stairs were a poor design and were very unstable. To reach the height needed for the 767s, the stairs had to be extremely long so they stuck out onto the ramp just waiting to be hit by a careless tug driver. The smallest puff of wind would cause them to sway making it difficult to walk up or down them especially if you were carrying your bags. Simply put, they were unsafe. They too found their way to our parking spots.

After making a few trips up and down these wobbly stairs and almost falling or dropping my bags I decided to take a stand. At some point in every pilot's career he will find himself in a situation where he is forced to decide between what the company wants and what is safe or legal. Liberal use of the word "safety" is generally recommended if you plan to butt heads with the company. If it ultimately comes down to a question of legality or ends up in a union grievance it is difficult for the company to take abusive action if it will make them look like they are willing to compromise safety to get what they want. In this situation I sincerely believed the stairs were unsafe and I didn't feel like I or my crew should have to be subject to the potential dangers of the faulty stairs.

My initial efforts included a safety report that had little effect but would have been required later if not submitted at the beginning. The first time I blocked in to a spot that had the rickety stairs after I filed my safety report I radioed operations to request a replacement of the stairs before deplaning or allowing ramp personnel onto the aircraft citing safety concerns. I was told they would look into it but the sort couldn't wait and the stairs weren't changed for that night's operations.

The next night as I approached the assigned parking spot I noticed the wobbly type of stairs waiting for us. I stopped the aircraft on the taxiway short of the parking spot and called ops on the radio and informed them that we wouldn't be able to accept the improper set of stairs due to safety concerns and asked if they wanted to assign another parking spot or switch the stairs before I blocked in.

A busy airport with hundreds of aircraft full of time sensitive material can't afford to have one of its taxiways blocked. The proper stairs were produced and we blocked in. Yes, I knew I had whacked the hornet's nest with a stick and I would certainly be visiting with the flight manager once I got inside but it had to be done.

As was expected, the hornets that were disturbed had raised holy heck with the flight manager complaining about the A300 Captain that had interrupted traffic flow on the ground and delayed the unloading of the aircraft. It was probably the case that those who complained weren't as upset about actual operational interruptions as much as having their importance questioned and the authority to govern their tiny portions of the kingdom challenged by a lowly pilot.

The flight manager had to deal with the uproar and do some research on the stairs since the term of safety had been invoked. According to the manufacturer's specifications those stairs were designed for and authorized for use on several aircraft models but the Airbus was not one of them. The ramp at Wilmington became a safer place as the proper air stairs were returned to the A300s. Unfortunately other stations throughout the system that had been Airborne before the merger still had the unwanted stairs so the victory was almost meaningless.

The aircraft mechanics at some of these stations suffered more than just the climb up a set of wobbly stairs. As DHL rearranged which of their two main contract carriers would service a given airport, they continually transferred the mechanics from one station to the next. Several of the mechanics resigned and looked for work where they were and a few kept their jobs and took the abuse of being transferred to a station not of their choosing for a duration that in some cases turned out to be rather short lived.

In reality, all of the employees were impacted by the move to the corn field. While most of the ramp employees at the DHL hub hadn't made the transition there were other key personnel that had, and they all were forced to move to Wilmington or make the three hour round trip from Cincinnati to get to work every day. It was still true that about seventy-five percent of the pilot group commuted to work from other parts of the country. When operating out of a major airport, commuting could be done on several of the various passenger carriers which serviced that airport. The travel options available to the commuting pilot at Wilmington were reduced to just Astar Air Cargo or ABX. Several pilots decided to move to Wilmington to avoid the extra complications of just getting to work. Many of the Astar crew members who chose to continue commuting to work would jump seat to Wilmington on ABX and the occasional Airborne pilot rode to work with us as well. The flight crews from both carriers treated each other respectfully and with professionalism for the most part even if the atmosphere in the cockpit seemed a little chilly at times.

A few of our crew members who rode to work on ABX aircraft shared stories of what they had observed at some of the Airborne facilities during their commutes. There were reports of station personnel who just couldn't accept that they were now DHL and no longer Airborne Express. They protested by refusing to use the new DHL packaging and continued to process shipments in the old gray Airborne envelopes. There were rumors of freight being trucked from station to station in order to inflate the volume to a level that could justify keeping an ABX aircraft operating out of a given station.

It's difficult to know just how much of what we were hearing was true but from what we could see at Wilmington it appeared that the ABX ground services were generating plenty of activity for which they could bill DHL. One service that can't be avoided in the winter is deicing and anti-icing of aircraft. To avoid excessive expense and use of deice fluid the system was set up on an as needed bases. If it was determined during preflight that the aircraft would need anti-icing a flight crew member would call and schedule it. In reality it was usually the case that by the time we got to the aircraft it had already been sprayed with deice fluid before we had the chance to evaluate the need. There was even a disabled aircraft parked on the ramp that had no engines and was obviously not in flying condition that got deiced on a regular basis. Airborne was billing DHL for each of these deice applications.

Being sprayed with anti-ice fluid too often is certainly a better problem to have than not getting sprayed when you need to be. Like anti-icing, most procedures in aviation were well defined and standardized giving the U.S. the best and safest air transportation system in the world. Even our engine starting, push back and taxi operations are conducted with standard call outs so that things will go safely and smoothly no matter where we are operating, except at Wilmington. Airborne had been operating out of the corn field by themselves for so long that they had gotten used to using their own nonstandard vernacular and refused to learn the standard terminology. It was as if we were operating out of Never Never Land and the kids didn't want to grow up.

A standard engine start and push back procedure would consist of the ground crew letting the cockpit crew know they were on the head set and ready for start and push. The cockpit crew would coordinate with the ground crew using proper terminology and structured communications to affect a safe and efficient engine start and aircraft push back before taxi. All of this was done to prevent ground personnel from being sucked into and ruining a perfectly good fifteen million dollar engine or being run over with the main gear and causing a delay for tire cleaning.

Instead of hearing the phrase, "Clear to start engines," I would hear, "Go ahead and spin her," or "Fire 'em up." When I would say, "Brakes released, you're cleared to push," I should have heard, "roger, cleared to push. What is your block time?" Block time is the aviation standard term for the time you left the blocks. Instead, I would hear, "Copy, what's your roll time?" There's no such thing as a "roll" time in aviation.

In the real world after hearing the ground crew say, "Clear to start engines," I would turn the rotating beacon on so that those around the aircraft would know we were about to start. The procedures called for me to then say, "Beacon on. Start one." That was said so that the ground crew member on the head set with me could let me know if the beacon was not working. All too often at Wilmington we would be ready for start and hear the scratching sounds of the ground person plugging in the head set and then we would hear them parroting what they had heard during other start procedures, "Beacon on, start one," indicating that they had no understanding of what was to be said by whom and for what purpose.

I complained to management about the improper terminology and procedures assuring them that I was not upset about the ground personnel stealing my lines but that I did have serious concerns about what appeared to be a severe lack of training. Unfortunately the management team at Astar could only pass the concerns along to the ABX side of airport operations where I'm sure it was promptly ignored.

The safety concerns of the Astar Air Cargo pilot group were not without cause. I don't think most of us were initially aware of the lack of proper fire fighting equipment at the airport. Every major airport I have ever seen has a fire department except Wilmington. Instead, they had a pickup truck that was manned by volunteers who were people that normally worked in the sort facility. I suppose that could be considered a benefit since it meant they were already at the airport in the event of a fire or mishap that should require the services of a pickup truck.

The pickup/fire truck was actually called into service once after a rejected takeoff by one of Astar's A300s. A rejected takeoff or RTO is the most dangerous maneuver in aviation. Part of the reason for that is the tremendous heat generated by the brakes that have to stop a heavy aircraft moving at close to takeoff velocity. Brake fires are not uncommon in these situations and the controllers in the tower at Wilmington saw the brakes glowing when the aircraft came to a stop. They told the flight crew that the brakes were on fire. The flight crew didn't know what side of the aircraft had the fire and not wanting to open a normal entry door that may be near a fire, the crew exited the aircraft through the front sliding windows using the inertia reels which are lines designed to lower a crew member to the ground in the event of an emergency. During the evacuation one crew member injured his ankle. The airport pickup truck was dispatched and might have even been helpful had it gotten there in time to let the crew know what side of the aircraft had the hot brake issue.

We had only been flying out of Wilmington for a couple of years and were still operating under the mistaken belief that some of the issues surrounding the airport could be fixed when we got word that DHL was considering shutting us down. At first we thought the reports were a scare tactic employed by the company to cause us to give in on certain issues during contract negotiations. Sadly that was not the case. Deutsche Post thought they were losing money on domestic package deliveries. They discontinued point to point domestic deliveries in the U.S. and concentrated on the international side of the business.

To their way of thinking it was not a result of the huge amounts of money spent on a new hub that was abandoned nor the infrastructure put into an aging airfield or even the cost of operating that airfield with a group of people that didn't want you there in the first place that had cost them the financial losses. They actually believed it was delivering packages in the U.S. that was responsible for them losing money. It was unclear if anyone from Deutsche Post even came over from Germany to see why they were hemorrhaging cash but it didn't matter. They had decided to save money by doing less business. To me it was tantamount to having a lawn mowing company and trying to save money by mowing fewer lawns. They could just as well have closed the entire business and saved a boat load of cash.

The dry desert air of the Southwestern United States is where aircraft go to die. They are taken there to be stored until they are needed again or chopped up for scrap. The Boeing 727s were the first of our aircraft to head west. Senior crew members could keep their job for a while and transition to the DC-8 but junior crew members were furloughed. The Airbuses would be the next to go to the desert and I would soon find myself without an airplane to fly.

By mid June of 2009 all of our 727s were gone and a couple of the A300s had already hit the sands of the Southwest. I was in one of the remaining Airbuses on a JFK weekend layover that included a Sunday afternoon trip back to Wilmington for the Sunday package sort which would be the last trip for which I was scheduled. Daytime flights for us were rare and enjoyable. It was a beautiful cloudless Sunday afternoon with great visibility. I landed and taxied to our parking spot. After I set the brake I shut down the engines and called for the parking checklist.

The air stairs were pulled up to the door as we gathered our belongings to exit the flight deck. I stepped out of the cockpit and turned to take a last look struggling to keep my emotions in check. At the foot of the air stairs I put my bags in the back of the crew van and turned to face the aircraft I had just landed. It was Sunday, June 21, 2009, the Summer Solstice, Father's Day and the day of the final round of the Men's U.S. Open Golf Tournament but none of that was important to me at that moment. I walked over to the airplane and patted it on the nose to say good bye knowing I had probably just made my last flight.

Chapter Nine

Bits And Pieces

DHL abandoned Wilmington and went back to Cincinnati. In 2013 they celebrated the opening of their new expanded hub at the Cincinnati Airport which is actually located in northern Kentucky. There were several DHL big wigs there as well as the Governor of Kentucky who of course was thrilled to have two of the three major overnight package businesses headquartered in his state. Few if any of the original employees that had made DHL a great company before its purchase by Deutsche Post were there to take part in the celebration.

DHL donated the airport at Wilmington to the Clinton County Port Authority in 2010. It was as if DHL said to Wilmington, "Sorry about your economy. Here....have a free airport."

The big question that remains is: Did any of this have to happen? Nobody but Deutsche Post wanted DHL to buy Airborne but they did and it is likely the case that if the employees at Airborne had just done their job, we would all probably still be working. Without DHL, Airborne was probably doomed anyway.

Of course we'll never know for sure but as it stands, the town of Wilmington is economically devastated with eighty percent of its population out of work and there is nothing to show for it all but an abandoned airport in the middle of a corn field.

Either way, aviation has left me behind. I almost feel like some of the airports I used to fly in and out of during my career that have now been closed. If you fly over Denver's Stapleton Airport or Austin's Meuller Airport now, all you can see are a few scars on the landscape that used to be runways. The rest has been overrun with subdivisions and shopping centers like so many weeds taking over what used to be a beautiful garden.

At least I no longer have to put up with the frustrations that plagued me on a daily basis while I was flying. Just getting into the building was problematic. Even though I was wearing my uniform and had my company ID badge prominently displayed I was forced to squeeze through a ridiculous turnstile to enter. Ten feet away trucks were driving in and out through an open gate. Worse than that, just a half mile down the road the airport perimeter fence consisted of a single piece of poorly strung barbed wire that my grand mother could have walked over. Most security measures accomplish little more than frustrate decent people while leaving open invitations to the bad guys.

At the new Denver airport they even made it difficult to get OUT of the secure area. When we flew into Denver and wanted to leave our facility to get to the van taking us to the hotel we had to find someone with a badge that would allow him to open the door for us to leave. Worse than that, his badge had to be of the type that allowed more than one person to exit during one door opening. I kid you not, most of the ID badges would only allow an employee to let just one person out at a time.

Most of what the government does to protect the traveling public is like the Wizard of Oz. They stand behind a curtain of activity generating a bunch of noise and flashing lights that are designed to look good but don't really accomplish much. One perfect example is the drug testing program. One would think that the testing would be done prior to a pilot making a flight so as to prevent them from flying while impaired. In fact, random testing is only done at the end of a duty period. They also test a flight crew member after an incident or accident. That way in those cases where alcohol or drugs are a factor, the accident won't have been prevented but at least the government will be able to say, "Ah ha! I told you so!"

It's also good to be done with those bumpy van rides to the hotel after a fourteen hour duty day. I don't miss unpacking, trying to sleep during the day and then repacking my suitcase just to catch another bumpy van ride to the airport to do it all again.

Truth be told all the semiannual flight physicals, recurrent training and simulator check rides were starting to wear a little thin on me as well. And nobody likes to update their approach plates every week. All that open the binder, take a page out, put a page in, close the binder repetition stuff really wears out your fingers.

Aw who am I kidding? I would gladly put up with all of that for just one more chance to be able to see the runway and approach lights magically appear in front of me when I break out of the clouds after shooting an instrument approach in heavy weather or feel the thrust push me back in my seat as I shove the throttles up for takeoff.

I may have suggested that DHL was only good for painting everything yellow but that's not true. They were able to put together one of the finest collection of aviation professionals anywhere and it was a privilege to have been able to fly with them.

Subsequent decisions by DHL may have scattered them to the four corners of the aviation world but it was wonderful while it lasted. Most of the younger ones are now flying for various carriers making a fraction of what they did at DHL/Astar. The old fossils like myself are retired and can only look back on our aviation career like Al Bundy recalling his high school football days telling the story of making four touchdowns in a single game. There are also those who have taken that final flight west that we all must take, most through natural causes but sadly a few by their own hand somehow not realizing there is life after DHL.

My life after aviation has been somewhat less than fulfilling. Nothing I've tried has been able to take the place of flying. I opened a chain of frozen yogurt shops. It was gratifying to see that my judgement about frozen yogurt being the next great thing was confirmed by thousands of other fro-yo fortune hunters who opened up shops on every street corner. Fortunately I was spared the indignity of having to watch my business being devoured by competition but only because I was forced to close my stores early due to some very severe legal complications on the part of the franchisor.

The most fun I have had since my flying days was hosting my radio show. I formed a production company to produce a show called "It's Just Business." The name comes from the phrase, "It's not personal, it's just business" which translated means "it doesn't matter if we're friends or not, I'm still going to take all of your money." It's a particularly fitting title because when you are in business for yourself that's exactly what people will be doing to you even though they're not actually saying it.

On the air I was The Business Crash Test Dummy and would help others avoid the mistakes I had made in business by sharing my experience through interviews with guest experts and discussing areas of business that a small business owner or operator would encounter.

The plan was to recover the cost of production and generate a profit through advertising revenue. That plan failed to gain any traction when the media group I had used to air my show placed me on a radio station that was giving air time away for free to those who advertised on their sister station. This experience enhanced my business education by teaching me that it can be terribly difficult to sell something that the guy next door is giving away for free. While my radio show is no longer being broadcast, my production company is still intact so I am perfectly positioned to take advantage of the opportunities when Hollywood calls me up to broadcast with the "big boys". It's always good to be prepared.

Now that I'm out of the sky and off of the air, I'm putting my wisdom on paper. I have two books to my credit so far. The first was a humor book that I wrote a few years ago and the second is the book you're reading now. With all of my business experience I should probably write a "how not to" book. I can call it "I Lost A Million Dollars In Business And You Can Too." Once all of my books start selling like they should, I'll be making more money than you can shake a stick at. Of course, until then I'm going to have to go back to work, so let me ask…. "Would you like fries with that?"

Made in the USA
Middletown, DE
15 January 2016